The Athelings
Or
The Three Gifts
Vol. 2

by

Margaret Oliphant

The Athelings
Or
The Three Gifts
Vol. 2
by Margaret Oliphant

ISBN: 978-93-59955-65-0

Published by

DOUBLE 9 BOOKS

2/13-B, Ansari Road
Daryaganj, New Delhi – 110002
info@double9books.com
www.double9books.com
Tel. 011-40042856

ABOUT THE AUTHOR

Margaret Oliphant Wilson Oliphant was a Scottish author and historical writer who usually wrote under the name Mrs. Oliphant. She was born Margaret Oliphant Wilson on April 4, 1828, and died on June 20, 1897. She writes "domestic realism, the historical novel, and tales of the supernatural" as her short stories. Margaret Oliphant was born in Wallyford, near Musselburgh, East Lothian. She was the only daughter and youngest child still living of Margaret Oliphant (c. 1789-17 September 1854) and Francis W. Wilson, a clerk. We lived in Lasswade, Glasgow, and Liverpool when she was a child. In Wallyford, a street called Oliphant Gardens is named after her. As a girl, she was always trying new things with writing. Passages in the Life of Mrs. Margaret Maitland, her first book, came out in 1849. This was about the mostly successful Scottish Free Church movement, which was something her folks agreed with. Next came Caleb Field in 1851, the same year she met publisher William Blackwood in Edinburgh and was asked to write for Blackwood's Magazine. She did so for the rest of her life and wrote over 100 articles, including one that criticized Arthur Dimmesdale in Nathaniel Hawthorne's "The Scarlet Letter."

CONTENTS

BOOK II

CHAPTER I
THE WILLOWS

The Willows was a large low house, with no architectural pretensions, but bright as villa could be upon the sunniest side of the Thames. The lawn sloped to the river, and ended in a deep fringe and border of willows, sweeping into the water; while half-way across the stream lay a little fairy island, half enveloped in the same silvery foliage, but with bowers and depths of leaves within, through which some stray sunbeam was always gleaming. The flower-beds on the lawn were in a flush with roses; the crystal roof of a large conservatory glistened in the sun. Flowers and sunshine, fragrance and stillness, the dew on the grass, and the morning light upon the river—no marvel that to eyes so young and inexperienced, this Richmond villa looked like a paradise on earth.

It was early morning—very early, when nobody seemed awake but themselves in the great house; and Agnes and Marian came down stairs softly, and, half afraid of doing wrong, stole out upon the lawn. The sun had just begun to gather those blobs of dew from the roses, but all over the grass lay jewels, bedded deep in the close-shorn sod, and shining in the early light. An occasional puff of wind came crisp across the river, and turned to the sun the silvery side of all those drooping willow-leaves, and the willows themselves swayed and sighed towards the water, and the water came up upon them now and then with a playful plunge and flow. The two girls said nothing to each other as they wandered along the foot of the slope, looking over to the island, where already the sun had penetrated to his nest of trees. All this simple beauty, which was not remarkable to the fashionable guests of Mrs Edgerley, went to the very heart of these simple children of Bellevue. It moved them to involuntary delight—joy which could give no reason, for they thought there had never been such a beautiful summer morning, or such a scene.

And by-and-by they began to talk of last night—last night, their first night at the Willows, their first entrance into the home life of "the great." They had no moral maxims at their finger-ends, touching the vanity of riches, nor had the private opinion entertained by Papa and Mamma, that "the country" paid for the folly of "the aristocracy," and that the science of Government was a mere piece of craft for the benefit of "the privileged classes," done any harm at all to the unpolitical imaginations of Agnes and Marian. They were scarcely at their ease yet, and were a great deal more timid than was comfortable; yet they took very naturally to this fairy life, and found an unfailing fund of wonder and admiration in it. They admired everything indeed, had a certain awe and veneration for everybody, and could not sufficiently admire the apparent accomplishments and real grace of their new associates.

"Agnes!—I wonder if there is anything I could learn?" said Marian, rather timidly; "everybody here can do something; it is very different from doing a little of everything, like Miss Tavistock at Bellevue—and we used to think her accomplished!—but do you think there is anything I could learn?"

"And me!" said Agnes, somewhat disconsolately.

"You? no, indeed, you do not need it," said Marian, with a little pride. "You can do what none of them can do;—but they can talk about everything these people, and every one of them can do something. There is that Sir Langham—you would think he was only a young gentleman—but Mrs Edgerley says he makes beautiful sketches. We did not understand people like these when we were at home."

"What do you think of Sir Langham, May?" asked Agnes seriously.

"Think of him? oh, he is very pleasant," said Marian, with a smile and a slight blush: "but never mind Sir Langham; do you think there is anything I could learn?"

"I do not know," said Agnes; "perhaps you could sing. I think you might sing, if you would only take courage and try."

"Sing! oh no, no!"; said Marian; "no one could venture to sing after the young lady—did you hear her name, Agnes?—who sang last night. She did not speak to any one, she was more by herself than we were. I wonder who she could be."

"Mrs Edgerley called her Rachel," said Agnes. "I did not hear any other name. I think it must be the same that Mrs Edgerley told mamma about; you remember she said——"

"I am here," said a low voice suddenly, close beside them. The girls started back, exceedingly confused and ashamed. They had not perceived a sort of little bower, woven among the willows, from which now hastily appeared the third person who spoke. She was a little older than Agnes, very slight and girlish in her person—very dark of complexion, with a magnificent mass of black hair, and large liquid dark eyes. Nothing else about her was remarkable; her features were small and delicate, her cheeks colourless, her very lips pale; but her eyes, which were not of a slumbrous lustre, but full of light, rapid, earnest, and irregular, lighted up her dark pallid face with singular power and attractiveness. She turned upon them quickly as they stood distressed and irresolute before her.

"I did not mean to interrupt you," said this new-comer; "but you were about to speak of me, and I thought it only honest to give you notice that I was here."

"Thank you," said Agnes with humility. "We are strangers, and did not know—we scarcely know any one here; and we thought you were nearly about our own age, and perhaps would help us—" Here Agnes stopped short; she was not skilled in making overtures of friendship.

"No, indeed no," cried their new acquaintance, hurriedly. "I never make friends. I could be of no use. I am only a dependent, scarcely so good as that. I am nothing here."

"And neither are we," said Agnes, following shyly the step which this strange girl took away from them. "We never were in a house like this before. We do not belong to great people. Mrs Edgerley asked us to come, because we met her at Mr Burlington's, and she has been very kind, but we know no one. Pray, do not go away."

The thoughtful eyes brightened into a sudden gleam. "We are called Atheling," said Marian, interposing in her turn. "My sister is Agnes, and I am Marian—and you Miss——"

"My name is Rachel," said their new friend, with a sudden and violent blush, making all her face crimson. "I have no other—call me so, and I will like it. You think I am of your age; but I am not like you—you do not know half so much as I know."

"No—that is very likely," said Agnes, somewhat puzzled; "but I think you do not mean education," said the young author immediately, seeing Marian somewhat disposed to resent on her behalf this broad assertion. "You mean distress and sorrow. But we have had a great deal of grief at home. We have lost dear little children, one after another. We are not ignorant of grief."

Rachel looked at them with strange observation, wonder, and uncertainty. "But you are ignorant of me—and I am ignorant of you," she said slowly, pausing between her words. "I suppose you mean just what you say, do you? and I am not much used to that. Do you know what I am here for?—only to sing and amuse the people—and you still want to make friends with me!"

"Mrs Edgerley said you were to be a singer, but you did not like it," said Marian; "and I think you are very right."

"Did she say so?—and what more?" said Rachel, smiling faintly. "I want to hear now, though I did not when I heard your voices first."

"She said you were a connection of the family," said Agnes.

The blood rushed again to the young stranger's brow. "Ah! I understand," she said; "she implied—yes. I know how she would do. And you will still be friends with *me*?"

At that moment it suddenly flashed upon the recollection of both the girls that Mamma had disapproved of this prospective acquaintance. They both blushed with instant consciousness, and neither of them spoke. In an instant Rachel became frozen into a haughtiness far exceeding anything within the power of Mrs Edgerley. Little and slight as she was, her girlish frame rose to the dignity of a young queen. Before Agnes could say a word, she had left them with a slight and lofty bow. Without haste, but with singular rapidity, she crossed the dewy lawn, and went into the house, acknowledging, with a stately inclination of her head, some one who passed her. The girls were so entirely absorbed, watching her progress, that they did not perceive who this other person was.

CHAPTER II
AN EMBARRASSING COMPANION

"Strange creature!" said Sir Langham Portland, who had joined the girls almost before they were aware; "Odd girl! If Lucifer had a sister, I should know where to find her; but a perfect siren so far as music is concerned. Did you hear her sing last night—that thing of Beethoven's—what is the name of it? Do you like Beethoven, though? *She*, I suppose, worships him."

"We know very little about music," said Marian. She thought it proper to make known the fact, but blushed in spite of herself, and was much ashamed of her own ignorance. Marian was quite distressed and impatient to find herself so much behind every one else.

"Oh!" said Sir Langham—which meant that the handsome guardsman was a good deal flattered by the blush, and did not care at all for the want of information—in fact, he was cogitating within himself, being no great master of the art of conversation, what to speak of next.

"I am afraid Miss—Rachel was not pleased," said Agnes; "we disturbed her here. I am afraid she will think we were rude."

"Eh!" said Sir Langham, with a look of astonishment. "Oh, don't trouble yourself—she's accustomed to that. Pretty place this. Suppose a fellow on the island over there, what a capital sketch he could make;—with two figures instead of three, the effect would be perfect!"

"We were two figures before you came," said Marian, turning half away, and with a smile.

"Ah! quite a different suggestion," said Sir Langham. "Your two figures were all white and angelical—maiden meditation—mine would be—Elysium. Happy sketcher! happier hero!—and you could not suppose a more appropriate scene."

But Agnes and Marian were much too shy and timid to answer this as they might have answered Harry Oswald under the same circumstances. Agnes half interrupted him, being somewhat in haste to change the conversation. "You are an artist yourself?" said Agnes.

"No," said Sir Langham; "not at all,—no more than everybody else is. I have no doubt you know a hundred people better at it than I."

"I do not think, counting every one," said Marian, "that we know a hundred, or the half of a hundred, people altogether; and none of them make sketches. Mrs Edgerley said yours were quite remarkable."

"A great many things are quite remarkable with Mrs Edgerley," said Sir Langham through his mustache. "But what an amazing circle yours must be! One must do something with one's spare time. That old fellow is the hardest rascal to kill of any I know—don't you find him so?"

"No—not when we are at home," said Marian.

"Ah! in the country, I suppose; and you are Lady Bountifuls, and attend to all the village," said Sir Langham. He had quite made up his mind that these young girls, who were not fashionable nor remarkable in any way, save for the wonderful beauty of the youngest, were daughters of some squire in Banburyshire, whom it was Lord Winterbourne's interest to do a service to.

"No, indeed, we have not any village—we are not Lady Bountifuls; but we do a great many things at home," said Marian. Something restrained them both, however, from their heroic purpose of declaring at once their "rank in life;" they shrank, with natural delicacy, from saying anything about themselves to this interrogator, and were by no means clear that it would be right to tell Sir Langham Portland that they lived in Bellevue.

"May we go through the conservatory, I wonder?" said Agnes;—the elder sister, remembering the parting charge of her mother, began to be somewhat uneasy about their handsome companion—he might possibly fall in love with Marian—that was not so very dreadful a hypothesis,— for Agnes was human, and did not object to see the natural enemies of womankind taken captive, subjugated, or even entirely slain. But Marian might fall in love with *him*! That was an appalling thought; two distinct lines of anxiety began to appear in Agnes's forehead; and the imagination of the young genius instantly called before her the most touching and pathetic picture, of a secret love and a broken heart.

"Marian, we may go into the conservatory," repeated Agnes; and she took her sister's hand and led her to where the Scotch gardener was opening the windows of that fairy palace. Sir Langham still gave them his attendance, following Marian as she passed through the ranks of flowers, and echoing her delight. Sir Langham was rather relieved to find them at last in enthusiasm about something. This familiar and well-known feature of young ladyhood set him much more at his ease.

And the gardener, with benign generosity, gathered some flowers for his young visitors. They thanked him with such thoroughly grateful thanks, and were so respectful of his superior knowledge, that this worthy functionary brightened under their influence. Sir Langham followed surprised and amused. He thought Marian's simple ignorance of all those delicate splendid exotic flowers, as pretty as he would have thought her acquaintance with them had she been better instructed; and when one of her flowers fell from her hand, lifted it up with the air of a paladin, and placed it in his breast. Marian, though she had turned aside, *saw* him do it by some mysterious perception—not of the eye—and blushed with a secret tremor, half of pleasure, half of amusement. Agnes regarded it a great deal more seriously. Agnes immediately discovered that it was time to go in. She was quite indifferent, we are grieved to say, to the fate of Sir Langham, and thought nothing of disturbing the peace of that susceptible young gentleman; but her protection and guardianship of Marian was a much more serious affair. Their windows were in the end of the house, and commanded no view—so Mrs Edgerley, with a hundred regrets, was grieved to tell them—but these windows looked over an orchard and a clump of chestnuts, where birds sang and dew fell, and the girls were perfectly contented with the prospect; they had three rooms—a dressing-room, and two pretty bedchambers—into all of which the morning sun threw a sidelong glance as he passed; and they had been extremely delighted with their pretty apartments last night.

"Well!" said Agnes, as they arranged their flowers and put them in water, "everything is very pretty, May, but I almost wish we were at home."

"Why?" said Marian; but the beautiful sister had so much perception of the case, that she did not look up, nor show any particular surprise.

"Why?—because—because people don't understand what we are, nor who we belong to, nor how different—— Marian, you know quite well what is the cause!"

"But suppose people don't want to know?" said Marian, who was provokingly calm and at her ease; "we cannot go about telling everybody— no one cares. Suppose we were to tell Sir Langham, Agnes? He would think we meant that he has to come to Bellevue; and I am sure you would not like to see him there!"

This was a very conclusive argument, but Agnes had made up her mind to be annoyed.

"And there was Rachel," said Agnes, "I wonder why just at that moment we should have thought of mamma—and now I am sure she will not speak to us again."

"Mamma did not think it quite proper," said Marian doubtfully;—"I am sure I cannot tell why—but we were very near making up friendship without thinking; perhaps it is better as it is."

"It is never proper to hurt any one's feelings—and she is lonely and neglected and by herself," said Agnes. "Mamma cannot be displeased when I tell her; and I will try all I can to-day to meet with Rachel again. I think Rachel would think better of our house than of the Willows. Though it is a beautiful place, it is not kindly; it never could look like home."

"Oh, nonsense! if we had it to ourselves, and they were all here!" cried Marian. That indeed was a paradisaical conception. Agnes's uneasy mood could not stand against such an idea, and she arranged her hair with renewed spirits, having quite given up for the moment all desire for going home.

CHAPTER III
SOCIETY

But Rachel did not join the party either in their drives, their walks, or their conversations. She was not to be seen during the whole day, either out of doors or in, and did not even make her appearance at the dinner-table; and Agnes could not so much as hear any allusion made to her except once, when Mrs Edgerley promised a new arrival, "some really good music," and launched forth in praise of an extraordinary little genius, whom nothing could excuse for concealing her gift from the world. But if Rachel did not appear, Sir Langham did, following Marian with his eyes when he could not follow in person, and hovering about the young beauty like a man bewitched. The homage of such a cavalier was not to be despised; in spite of herself, the smile and the blush brightened upon the sweet face of Marian—she was pleased—she was amused—she was grateful to Sir Langham—and besides had a certain mischievous pleasure in her power over him, and loved to exercise the sway of despotism. Marian new little about coquetry, though she had read with attention Mrs Edgerley's novel on the subject; but, notwithstanding, had "a way" of her own, and some little practice in tantalising poor Harry Oswald, who was by no means so superb a plaything as the handsome guardsman. The excitement and novelty of her position—the attentions paid to her—the pretty things around her—even her own dress, which never before had been so handsome, brightened, with a variable and sweet illumination, the beauty which needed no aggravating circumstance. Poor Sir Langham gave himself up helpless and unresisting, and already, in his honest but somewhat slow imagination, made formal declarations to the supposititious Banburyshire Squire.

Agnes meanwhile sat by Marian's side, rather silent, eagerly watching for the appearance of Rachel—for now it was evening, and the really good music could not be long deferred, if it was to come to-night. Agnes was not neglected, though she had no Sir Langham to watch her movements. Mrs Edgerley herself came to the young genius now and then to introduce some one who was "dying to know the author of *Hope Hazlewood*;" and half disconcerted, half amused, Agnes began to feel herself entering upon the enjoyment of her reputation. No one could possibly suppose anything more different from the fanciful and delicate fame which charms the young poetic mind with imaginary glories, than these drawing-room compliments and protestations of interest and delight, to which, at first with a deep blush and overpowering embarrassment, and by-and-by with an uneasy consciousness of something ridiculous, the young author sat still and listened. The two sisters kept always close together, and had not courage enough to move from the corner in which they had first established themselves. Agnes, for the moment, had become the reigning whim in the brain of Mrs Edgerley. She came to her side now and then to whisper a few words of caressing encouragement, or to point out to her somebody of note; and when she left her young guest, Mrs Edgerley flew at once to the aforesaid somebody to call his or her attention to the pair of sisters, one of whom had *such* genius, and the other *such* beauty. Marian, occupied with her own concerns, took all this very quietly. Agnes grew annoyed, uneasy, displeased; she did not remember that she had once been mortified at the neglect of her pretty hostess, nor that Mrs Edgerley's admiration was as evanescent as her neglect. She began to think everybody was laughing at her claims to distinction, and that she amused the people, sitting here uneasily receiving compliments, immovable in her chair—and she was extremely grateful to Mr Agar, her former acquaintance, when he came, looking amused and paying no compliments, to talk to her, and to screen her from observation. Mr Agar had been watching her uneasiness, her embarrassment, her self-annoyance. He was quite pleased with the "study;" it pleased him as much as a *Watteau*, or a cabinet of old china; and what could connoisseur say more?

"You must confide your annoyance to me. I am your oldest acquaintance," said Mr Agar. "What has happened? Has your pretty sister been naughty—eh? or are all the people *so* much delighted with your book?"

"Yes," said Agnes, holding down her head a little, with a momentary shame that her two troubles should have been so easily found out.

"And why should they not be delighted?" said the ancient beau. "You would have liked me a great deal better had I been the same, when I first saw you; do you not like it now?"

"No," said Agnes.

"Yes; no. Your eyes do not talk in monosyllables," said the old gentleman, "eh? What has poor Sir Langham done to merit that flash of dissatisfaction? and I wonder what is the meaning of all these anxious glances towards the door?"

"I was looking for—for the young lady they call Rachel," said Agnes. "Do you know who she is, sir?—can you tell me? I am afraid she thought we were rude this morning, when we met her; and I wish very much to see her to-night."

"Ah! I know nothing of the young lady, but a good deal of the voice," said Mr Agar; "a fine soprano,—a good deal of expression, and plenty of fire. Yes, she needs nothing but cultivation to make a great success."

"I think, sir," said Agnes, suddenly breaking in upon this speech, "if you would speak to Mrs Edgerley for her, perhaps they would not teaze her about being a singer. She hates it. I know she does; and it would be very good of you to help her, for she has no friends."

Mr Agar looked at the young pleader with a smile of surprised amusement. "And why should I interfere on her behalf? and why should she not be a singer? and how do you suppose I could persuade myself to do such an injury to Art?"

"She dislikes it very much," said Agnes. "She is a woman—a girl—a delicate mind; it would be very cruel to bring her before the world; and indeed I am sure if you would speak to Mrs Edgerley—"

"My dear young lady," cried Mr Agar, with a momentary shrug of his eyebrows, and look of comic distress, "you entirely mistake my *rôle*. I am not a knight-errant for the rescue of distressed princesses. I am a humble servant of the beautiful; and a young lady's tremors are really not cause enough to induce me to resign a fine soprano. No. I bow before my fair enslavers," said the ancient Corydon, with a reverential obeisance, which belonged, like his words, to another century; "but my true and only mistress is Art."

Agnes was silenced in a moment; but whether by this declaration, or by the entrance of Rachel, who suddenly appeared, gliding in at a side-door, could not be determined. Rachel came in, so quickly, and with such a gliding motion, that anybody less intently on the watch could not have discovered the moment of her appearance. She was soon at the piano, and heard immediately; but she came there in a miraculous manner to all the other observers, as if she had dropped from heaven.

And while the connoisseur stood apart to listen undisturbed, and Mrs Edgerley's guests were suddenly stayed in their flutter of talk and mutual criticism by the "really good music" which their hostess had promised them, Agnes sat listening, moved and anxious,—not to the song, but to the singer. She thought the music—pathetic, complaining, and resentful—instead of being a renowned *chef-d'œuvre* of a famous composer, was the natural outcry of this lonely girl. She thought she could hear the solitary heart, the neglected life, making its appeal indignant and sorrowful to some higher ear than all these careless listeners. She bent unconsciously towards the singer, forgetting all her mother's rules of manners, and, leaning forward, supported her rapt and earnest face with her hand. Mrs Edgerley paused to point out to some one the sweet enthusiasm, the delightful impressionable nature of her charming young friend; but to tell the truth, Agnes was not thinking at all of the music. It seemed to her a strange impassioned monologue,—a thing of which she was the sole hearer,—an irrepressible burst of confidence, addressed to the only one here present who cared to receive the same.

When it was over she raised herself almost painfully from her listening posture; *she* did not join in any of the warm expressions of delight which burst from her neighbours; and with extreme impatience Agnes listened to the cool criticism of Mr Agar, who was delivering his opinion very near her. Her heart ached as she saw the musician turn haughtily aside, and heard her say, "I am here when you want me again;" and Rachel withdrew to a sofa in a corner, and, shading her delicate small face entirely with her hand, took up a book and read, or pretended to read. Agnes looked on with eager interest, while several people, one after another, approached the singer to offer her some of the usual compliments, and retreated immediately, disconcerted by their reception. Leaning back in her corner, with her book held obstinately before her, and the small pale hand shading the delicate face, it was impossible to intrude upon Rachel. Agnes sat watching her, quite absorbed and sad—thinking in her own quick creative mind, many a proud thought for Rachel—and fancying she could read in that unvarying and statue-like attitude a world of tumultuous feelings. She was so much occupied that she took no notice of Sir Langham; and even Marian, though she appealed to her twenty times, did not get more than a single word in reply.

"Is she not the most wonderful little genius?" cried Mrs Edgerley, making one of her sudden descents upon Agnes. "I tell everybody she is next to you—quite next to you in talent. I expect she will make quite a *furor* next season when she makes her *début*."

"But she dislikes it so much," said Agnes.

"What, music? Oh, you mean coming out: poor child, she does not know what is for her own advantage," said Mrs Edgerley. "My love, in *her* circumstances, people have no right to consult their feelings; and a successful singer may live quite a fairy life. Music is so entrancing—these sort of people make fortunes immediately, and then, of course, she could retire, and be as private as she pleased. Oh, yes, I am sure she will be delighted to gratify you, Mr Agar: she will sing again."

It scarcely required a word from Mrs Edgerley—scarcely a sign. Rachel seemed to know by intuition when she was wanted, and, putting down her book, went to the piano again;—perhaps Agnes was not so attentive this time, for she felt herself suddenly roused a few minutes after by a sudden tremor in the magnificent voice—a sudden shake and tremble, having the same effect upon the singing which a start would have upon the frame. Agnes looked round eagerly to see the cause—there was no cause apparent—and no change whatever in the company, save for the pale spasmodic face of Lord Winterbourne, newly arrived, and saluting his daughter at the door.

Was it this? Agnes could not wait to inquire, for immediately the music rose and swelled into such a magnificent burst and overflow that every one held his breath. To the excited ear of Agnes, it sounded like a glorious challenge and defiance, irrestrainable and involuntary; and ere the listeners had ceased to wonder, the music was over, and the singer gone.

"A sudden effect—our young performer is not without dramatic talent," said Mr Agar. Agnes said nothing; but she searched in the corner of the sofa with her eyes, watched the side-door, and stole sidelong looks at Lord Winterbourne. He never seemed at his ease, this uncomfortable nobleman; he had a discomfited look to-night, like a man defeated, and Agnes could not help thinking of Charlie, with his sudden enmity, and the old acquaintance of her father, and all the chances connected with Aunt Bridget's bequest; for the time, in her momentary impulse of dislike and repulsion, she thought her noble neighbour, ex-minister and peer of the realm as he was, was not a match for the big boy.

"Agnes, somebody says Lord Winterbourne is her father—Rachel's father—and she cannot bear him. Was that what Mrs Edgerley meant?" whispered Marian in her ear with a look of sorrow. "Did you hear her voice tremble—did you see how she went away? They say she is his daughter— oh, Agnes, can it be true?"

But Agnes did not know, and could not answer: if it was true, then it was very certain that Rachel must be right; and that there were depths and mysteries and miseries of life, of which, in spite of all their innocent acquaintance with sorrow, these simple girls had scarcely heard, and never knew.

CHAPTER IV
MAKING FRIENDS

The next morning, and the next again, Agnes and Marian vainly sought the little bower of willows looking for Rachel. Once they saw her escape hastily out of the shrubbery as they returned from their search, and knew by that means that she wished to avoid them; but though they heard her sing every night, they made no advance in their friendship, for that was the only time in which Rachel was visible, and then she defied all intrusion upon her haughty solitude. Mr Agar himself wisely kept aloof from the young singer. The old gentleman did not choose to subject himself to the chance of a repulse.

But if Rachel avoided them, Sir Langham certainly did not. This enterprising youth, having discovered their first early walk, took care to be in the way when they repeated it, and on the fourth morning, without saying anything to each other, the sisters unanimously decided to remain within the safe shelter of their own apartments. From a corner of their window they could see Sir Langham in vexation and impatience traversing the slope of the lawn, and pulling off the long ashy willow-leaves to toss them into the river. Marian laughed to herself without giving a reason, and Agnes was very glad they had remained in the house; but the elder sister, reasoning with elaborate wisdom, made up her mind to ask no further questions about Sir Langham, how Marian liked him, or what she thought of his attentions. Agnes thought too many inquiries might "put something into her head."

Proceeding upon this astute line of policy, Agnes took no notice whatever of all the assiduities of the handsome guardsman, not even his good-natured and brotherly attentions to herself. They were only to remain a fortnight at the Willows—very little harm, surely, could be done in that time, and they had but a slender chance of meeting again. So the elder sister, in spite of her charge of Marian, quieted her conscience and her fears—and in the mean time the two girls, with thorough and cordial simplicity, took pleasure in their holiday, finding everybody kind to them, and excusing with natural humbleness any chance symptom of neglect.

They had been a week at the Willows, and every day had used every means in their power to see Rachel again, when one morning, suddenly, without plot or premeditation, Agnes encountered her in a long passage which ran from the hall to the morning-room of Mrs Edgerley. There was a long window at the end of this passage, against which the small rapid figure, clothed in a dark close-fitting dress, without the smallest relief of ornament, stood out strangely, outlined and surrounded by the light. Agnes had some flowers in her hand, the gift of her acquaintance the gardener. She fancied that Rachel glanced at them wistfully, and she was eager of the opportunity. "They are newly gathered—will you take some?" said Agnes, holding out her hands to her. The young stranger paused, and looked for an instant distrustfully at her and the flowers. Agnes hoped nothing better than to be dismissed with a haughty word of thanks; but while Rachel lingered, the door of the morning-room was opened, and an approaching footstep struck upon the tiled floor. The young singer did not look behind her, did not pause to see who it was, but recognising the step, as it seemed, with a sudden start and tremor, suddenly laid her hand on Agnes's arm, and drew her hurriedly in within a door which she flung open. As soon as they were in, Rachel closed the door with haste and force, and stood close by it with evident agitation and excitement. "I beg your pardon—but hush, do not speak till he is past," she said in a whisper. Agnes, much discomposed and troubled, went to the window, as people generally do in embarrassment, and looked out vacantly for a moment upon the kitchen-garden and the servants' "offices," the only prospect visible from it. She could not help sharing a little the excitement of her companion, as she thought upon her own singular position here, and listened with an involuntary thrill to the slow step of the unknown person from whom they had fled, pacing along the long cool corridor to pass this door.

But he did not pass the door; he made a moment's pause at it, and then entered, coming full upon Rachel as she stood, agitated and defiant, close upon the threshold. Agnes scarcely looked round, yet she could see it was Lord Winterbourne.

"Good morning, Rachel. I trust you get on well here," said the new-comer in a soft and stealthy tone: "is this your sitting-room? Ah, bare enough, I see. Your are in splendid voice, I am glad to hear; some one is coming to-night, I understand, whose good opinion is important. You must take care to do yourself full justice. Are you well, child?"

He had approached close to her, and bestowed a cold kiss upon the brow which burned under his touch. "Perfectly well," said Rachel, drawing back with a voice unusually harsh and clear. Her agitation and excitement had for the moment driven all the music from her tones.

"And your brother is quite well, and all going on in the usual way at Winterbourne," continued the stranger. "I expect to have the house very full in a few weeks, and you must arrange with the housekeeper where to bestow yourselves. *You*, of course, I shall want frequently. As for Louis, I suppose he does nothing but fish and mope as usual. I have no desire to see more than I can help of *him*."

"There is no fear; his desire is as strong as yours," cried Rachel suddenly, her face varying from the most violent flush to a sudden passionate paleness. Lord Winterbourne answered by his cold smile of ridicule.

"I know his amiable temper," he said. "Now, remember what I have said about to-night. Do yourself justice. It will be for your advantage. Good-by. Remember me to Louis."

The door opened again, and he was gone. Rachel closed it almost violently, and threw herself upon a chair. "We owe him no duty—none. I will not believe it," cried Rachel. "No—no—no—I do not belong to him! Louis is not his!"

All this time, in the greatest distress and embarrassment, Agnes stood by the window, grieved to be an unwilling listener, and reluctant to remind Rachel of her presence by going away. But Rachel had not forgotten that she was there. With a sudden effort this strange solitary girl composed herself and came up to Agnes. "Do you know Lord Winterbourne?" she said quickly; "have you heard of him before you came here?"

"I think—— but, indeed, I may be mistaken," said Agnes timidly; "I think papa once knew him long ago."

"And did he think him a good man?" said Rachel.

This was a very embarrassing question. Agnes turned away, retreated uneasily, blushed, and hesitated. "He never speaks of him; I cannot tell," said Agnes.

"Do you know," said Rachel, eagerly, "they say he is my father—Louis's father; but we do not believe it, neither I nor he."

To this singular statement Agnes made no answer, save by a look of surprise and inquiry; the frightful uncertainty of such a position as this was beyond the innocent comprehension of Agnes Atheling. She looked with a blank and painful surprise into her young companion's face.

"And I will not sing to-night; I will not, because he bade me!" said Rachel. "Is it my fault that I can sing? but I am to be punished for it; they make me come to amuse them; and they want me to be a public singer. I should not care," cried the poor girl suddenly, in a violent burst of tears, passing from her passion and excitement to her natural character—"I would not mind it for myself, if it were not for Louis. I would do anything they bade me myself; I do not care, nothing matters to me; but Louis—Louis! he thinks it is disgrace, and it would break his heart!"

"Is that your brother?" said Agnes, bending over her, and endeavouring to soothe her excitement. Rachel made no immediate answer.

"He has disgrace enough already, poor boy," said Rachel. "We are nobody's children; or we are Lord Winterbourne's; and he who might be a king's son—and he has not even a name! Yes, he is my brother, my poor Louis: we are twins; and we have nobody but each other in the whole world."

"If he is as old as you," said Agnes, who was only accustomed to the usages of humble houses, and knew nothing of the traditions of a noble race, "you should not stay at Winterbourne: a man can always work—you ought not to stay."

"Do you think so?" cried Rachel eagerly. "Louis says so always, and I beg and plead with him. When he was only eighteen he ran away: he went and enlisted for a soldier—a common man—and was away a year, and then they bought him off, and promised to get him a commission; and I made him promise to me—perhaps it was selfish, for I could not live when he was gone—I made him promise not to go away again. And there he is at Winterbourne. I know you never saw any one like him; and now all these heartless people are going there, and Lord Winterbourne is afraid of him, and never will have him seen, and the whole time I will be sick to the very heart lest he should go away."

"But I think he ought to go away," said Agnes gravely.

Her new friend looked up in her face with an earnest and trembling scrutiny. This poor girl had a great deal more passion and vehemence in her character than had ever been called for in Agnes, but, an uninstructed and ill-trained child, knew nothing of the primitive independence, and had never been taught to think of right and wrong.

"We have a little house there," said Agnes, with a sudden thought. "Do you know the Old Wood Lodge? Papa's old aunt left it to him, and they say it is very near the Hall."

At the name Rachel started suddenly, rose up at once with one of her quick inconsiderate movements, and, throwing her arms round Agnes, kissed her cheek. "I knew I ought to know you," said Rachel, "and yet I did not think of the name. Dear old Miss Bridget, she loved Louis. I am sure she loved him; and we know every room in the house, and every leaf on the trees. If you come there, we will see you every day."

"We are coming there—and my mother," said Agnes. "I know you will be pleased to see mamma," said the good girl, her face brightening, and her eyes filling in spite of herself; "every one thinks she is like their own mother—and when you come to us you will think you are at home."

"We never had any mother," said Rachel, sadly; "we never had any home; we do not know what it is. Look, this is my home here."

Agnes looked round the large bare apartment, in which the only article of furniture worth notice was an old piano, and which looked only upon the little square of kitchen-garden and the servants' rooms. It was somewhat larger than both the parlours in Bellevue, and for a best room would have rejoiced Mrs Atheling's ambitious heart; but Agnes was already a little wiser than she had been in Islington, and it chilled her heart to compare this lonely and dreary apartment with all the surrounding luxuries, which Rachel saw and did not share.

"Come up with me and see Marian," said Agnes, putting her arm through her companion's; "you are not to avoid us now any more; we are all to be friends after to-day."

And Rachel, who did not know what friendship was, yielded, thinking of Louis. Had she been wrong throughout in keeping him, by her entreaties, so long at Winterbourne? A vision of a home, all to themselves, burst once in a great delight upon the mind of Rachel. If Louis would only consent to it! With such a motive before her as that, the poor girl fancied she "would not mind" being a singer after all.

CHAPTER V
CONFIDENTIAL

When the first ice was broken, Rachel became perfectly confidential with her new friends—*perfectly* confidential—far more so than they, accustomed to the domestic privateness of humble English life, could understand. This poor girl had no restraint upon her for family pride or family honour; no compensation in family sympathy; and her listeners, who had very little skill in the study of character, though one of them had written a novel, were extremely puzzled with a kind of doubleness, perfectly innocent and unconscious, which made Rachel's thoughts and words at different moments like the words and the thoughts of two different people. At one time she was herself, humble, timid, and content to do anything which any authority bade her do; but in a moment she remembered Louis; and the change was instantaneous—she became proud, stately, obdurate, even defiant. She was no longer herself, but the shadow and representative of her brother; and in this view Rachel resisted and defied every influence, anchoring her own wavering will upon Louis, and refusing, with unreasonable and unreasoning obstinacy, all injunctions and all persuasions coming from those to whom her brother was opposed. She seemed, indeed, to have neither plan nor thought for herself: Louis was her inspiration. *She* seemed to have been born for no other purpose but to follow, to love, and to serve this brother, who to her was all the world. As she sat on the pretty chintz sofa in that sunny little dressing-room where Agnes and Marian passed the morning, running rapidly over the environs of the Old Wood Lodge, and telling them about their future neighbours, they were amazed and amused to find the total absence of personal opinion, and almost of personal liking, in their new acquaintance. She had but one standard, to which she referred everything, and that was Louis. They saw the very landscape, not as it was, but as it appeared to this wonderful brother. They became acquainted with the village and its inhabitants through the medium of Louis's favourites and Louis's aversions. They were young enough and simple enough themselves to be perfectly ready to invest any unknown ideal person with all the gifts of fancy; and Louis immediately leaped forth from the unknown world, a presence and an authority to them both.

"The Rector lives in the Old Wood House," said Rachel, for the first time pausing, and looking somewhat confused in her rapid summary. "I am sure I do not know what to think—but Louis does not like him. I suppose you will not like him; and yet,"—here a little faint colour came upon the young speaker's pale face—"sometimes I have fancied he would have been a friend if we had let him; and he is quite sure to like you."

Saying this, she turned a somewhat wistful look upon Agnes—blushing more perceptibly, but with no sunshine or brightness in her blush. "Yes," said Rachel slowly, "he will like you—he will do for you; and you," she added, turning with sudden eagerness to Marian, "you are for Louis—remember! You are not to think of any one else till you see Louis. You never saw any one like him; he is like a prince to look at, and I know he is a great genius. Your sister shall have the Rector, and Louis shall be for you."

All this Rachel said hurriedly, but with the most perfect gravity, even with a tinge of sadness—grieved, as they could perceive, that her brother did not like the Rector, but making no resistance against a doom so unquestionable as the dislike of Louis: but her timid heart was somehow touched upon the subject; she became thoughtful, and lingered over it with a kind of melancholy pleasure. "Perhaps Louis might come to like him if he was connected with *you*," said Rachel meditatively; and the faint colour wavered and flickered on her face, and at last passed away with a low but very audible sigh.

"But they are all Riverses," she continued, in her usual rapid way. "The Rector of Winterbourne is always a Rivers—it is the family living; and if Lord Winterbourne's son should die, I suppose Mr Lionel would be the heir. His sister lives with him, quite an old lady: and then there is another Miss Rivers, who lives far off, at Abingford all the way. Did you ever hear of Miss Anastasia? But she does not call herself Miss—only the Honourable Anastasia Rivers. Old Miss Bridget was once her governess. Lord Winterbourne will never permit her to see us; but I almost think Louis would like to be friends with her, only he will not take the trouble. They are not at all friends with her at Winterbourne."

"Is she a relation?" said Agnes. The girls by this time were so much interested in the family story that they did not notice this admirable reason for the inclination of Louis towards this old lady unknown.

"She is the old lord's only child," said Rachel. "The old lord was Lord Winterbourne's brother, and he died abroad, and no one knew anything about him for a long time before he died. We want very much to hear about him; indeed, I ought not to tell you—but Louis thinks perhaps he knew something about us. Louis will not believe we are Lord Winterbourne's children; and though we are poor disgraced children any way, and though he hates the very name of Rivers, I think he would almost rather we belonged to the old lord; for he says," added Rachel with great seriousness, "that one cannot hate one's father, if he is dead."

The girls drew back a little, half in horror; but though she spoke in this rebellious fashion, there was no consciousness of wrong in Rachel's innocent and quiet face.

"And we have so many troubles," burst forth the poor girl suddenly. "And I sometimes sit and cry all day, and pray to God to be dead. And when anybody is kind to me," she continued, some sudden remembrance moving her to an outburst of tears, and raising the colour once more upon her colourless cheek, "I am so weak and so foolish, and would do anything they tell me. *I* do not care, I am sure, what I do—it does not matter to me; but Louis—no, certainly, I will not sing to-night."

"I wish very much," said Agnes, with an earnestness and courage which somewhat startled Marian—"I wish very much you could come home with us to our little house in Bellevue."

"Yes," said Marian doubtfully; but the younger sister, though she shared the generous impulse, could not help a secret glance at Agnes—an emphatic reminder of Mamma.

"No, I must make no friends," said Rachel, rising under the inspiration of Louis's will and injunctions. "It is very kind of you, but I must not do it. Oh, but remember you are to come to Winterbourne, and I will try to bring Louis to see you; and I am sure you know a great deal better, and could talk to him different from me. Do you know," she continued solemnly, "they never have given me any education at all, except to sing? I have never been taught anything, nor indeed Louis either, which is much worse than me— only he is a great genius, and can teach himself. The Rector wanted to help him; that is why I am always sure, if Louis would let him, he would be a friend."

And again a faint half-distinguishable blush came upon Rachel's face. No, it meant nothing, though Agnes and Marian canvassed and interpreted after their own fashion this delicate suffusion; it only meant that the timid gentle heart might have been touched had there been room for more than Louis; but Louis was supreme, and filled up all.

CHAPTER VI
THREE FRIENDS

That night, faithful to her purpose, Rachel did not appear in the drawing-room. How far her firmness would have supported her, had she been left to herself, it is impossible to tell; but she was not left to herself. "Mrs Edgerley came, saying just the same things as Lord Winterbourne," said Rachel, "and I knew I should be firm. Louis cannot endure Mrs Edgerley." She said this with the most entire unconsciousness that she revealed the whole motive and strength of her resistance in the words. Rachel, indeed, was perfectly unaware of the entire subjection in which she kept even her thoughts and her affections to her brother; but she could not help a little anxiety and a little nervousness as to whether "Louis would like" her new acquaintances. She herself brightened wonderfully under the influence of these companions—expanded out of her dull and irritable solitude, and with girlish eagerness forecast their fortunes, seizing at once, in idea, upon Marian as the destined bride of Louis, and with a voluntary self-sacrifice making over, with a sigh and a secret thrill of pride, the only person who had ever wakened any interest in her own most sisterly bosom, to Agnes. She pleased herself greatly with these visions, and built them on a foundation still more brittle than that of Alnaschar—for it was possible that all her pleasant dreams might be thrown into the dust in a moment, if—dreadful possibility!—"Louis did not like" these first friends of poor Rachel's youth.

And when she brightened under this genial influence, and softened out of the haughtiness and solitary state which, indeed, was quite foreign to her character, Rachel became a very attractive little person. Even the sudden change in her sentiments and bearing when she returned to her old feeling of representing Louis, added a charm. Her large eyes troubled and melting, her pale small features which were very fine and regular, though so far from striking, her noble little head and small pretty figure, attracted in the highest degree the admiration of her new friends. Marian, who rather suspected that she herself was rather pretty, could not sufficiently admire the grace and refinement of Rachel; and Agnes, though candidly admitting that there was "scarcely any one" so beautiful as Marian, notwithstanding bestowed a very equal share of her regard upon the attractions of their companion.

And the trio fell immediately into all the warmth of girlish friendship. The Athelings went to visit Rachel in her great bare study, and Rachel came to visit them in their pretty little dressing-room; and whether in that sun-bright gay enclosure, or within the sombre and undecorated walls of the room which looked out on the kitchen-garden, a painter would have been puzzled to choose which was the better scene. They were so pretty a group anywhere—so animated—so full of eager life and intelligence—so much disposed to communicate everything that occurred to them, that Rachel's room brightened under the charm of their presence as she herself had done. And this new acquaintanceship made a somewhat singular revolution in the drawing-room—where the young musician, after her singing, was instantly joined by her two friends. She was extremely reserved and shy of every one else, and even of them occasionally, under the eyes of Mrs Edgerley; but she was no longer the little tragical princess who buried herself in the book and the corner, and neither heard nor saw anything going around her. And the fact that they had some one whose position was even more doubtful and uneasy than their own, to give heart and courage to, animated Agnes and Marian, as nothing else could have done. They recovered their natural spirits, and were no longer overawed by the great people surrounding them; they had so much care for Rachel that they forgot to be self-conscious, or to trouble themselves with inquiries touching their own manners and deportment, and what other people thought of the same; and on the whole, though their simplicity was not quite so amusing as at first, "other people" began to have a kindness for the fresh young faces, always so honest, cloudless, and sincere.

But Agnes's "reputation" had died away, and left very little trace behind it. Mrs Edgerley had found other lions, and at the present moment held in delusion an unfortunate young poet, who was much more like to be harmed by the momentary idolatry than Agnes. The people who had been dying to know the author of *Hope Hazlewood*, had all found out that the shy young genius did not talk in character—had no gift of conversation, and, indeed, did nothing at all to keep up her fame; and if Agnes chanced to feel a momentary mortification at the prompt desertion of all her admirers, she wisely kept the pang to herself, and said nothing about it. They were not neglected—for the accomplished authoress of *Coquetry* and the *Beau Monde* had some kindness at her heart after all, and had always a smile to spare for her young guests when they came in her way; they were permitted to roam freely about the gardens and the conservatory; they were by no means hindered in their acquaintance with Rachel, whom Mrs Edgerley was really much disposed to bring out and patronise; and one of them, the genius or the beauty, as best suited her other companions, was not unfrequently honoured with a place in Mrs Edgerley's barouche—a pretty shy lay figure in that rustling, radiant, perfumy *bouquet* of fine ladies, who talked over her head about things and people perfectly unknown to the silent auditor, and impressed her with a vague idea that this elegant and easy gossip was brilliant "conversation," though it did not quite sound, after all, like that grand unattainable conversation to be found in books. After this fashion, liking their novel life wonderfully well, and already making a home of that sunny little dressing-room, they drew gradually towards the end of their fortnight. As yet nothing at all marvellous had happened to them, and even Agnes seemed to have forgotten the absolute necessity of letting everybody know that they "did not belong to great people," but instead of a rural Hall, or Grange of renown, lived only in Number Ten, Bellevue.

CHAPTER VII
A TERRIBLE EVENT

For Agnes, we are grieved to confess, had fallen into all the sudden fervour of a most warm and enthusiastic girlish friendship. She forgot to watch over her sister, though Mrs Atheling's letters did not fail to remind her of her duty; she forgot to ward off the constant regards of Sir Langham. She began to be perfectly indifferent and careless of the superb sentinel who mounted guard upon Marian every night. For the time, Agnes was entirely occupied with Rachel, and with the new world so full of a charmed unknown life, which seemed to open upon them all in this Old Wood Lodge; she spent hours dreaming of some discovery which might change the position of the unfortunate brother and sister; she took up with warmth and earnestness their dislike to Lord Winterbourne. If it sometimes occurred to her what a frightful sentiment this was on the part of children to their father, she corrected herself suddenly, and declared in her own mind, with heart and energy, that he could not be their father—that there was no resemblance between them. But this, it must be confessed, was a puzzling subject, and offered continual ground for speculation; for princes and princesses, stolen away in their childhood, were extremely fictitious personages, even to an imagination which had written a novel; and Agnes could not help a thrill of apprehension when she thought of Louis and Marian, of the little romance which Rachel had made up between them, and how her own honourable father and mother would look upon this unhappy scion of a noble house— this poor boy who had no name.

This future, so full of strange and exciting possibilities, attracted with an irresistible power the imaginative mind of Agnes. She went through it chapter by chapter—through earnest dialogues, overpowering emotions, many a varying and exciting scene. The Old Wood Lodge, the Old Wood House, the Hall, the Rector, the old Miss Rivers, the unknown hero, Louis—these made a little private world of persons and places to the vivid imagination of the young dreamer. They floated down even upon Mrs Edgerley's drawing-room, extinguishing its gay lights, its pretty faces, and its hum of conversation; but with still more effect filled all her mind and meditations, as she rested, half reclining, upon the pretty chintz sofa in the pretty dressing-room, in the sweet summer noon with which this sweet repose was so harmonious and suitable. The window was open, and the soft wind blowing in fluttered all the leaves of that book upon the little table, which the sunshine, entering too, brightened into a dazzling whiteness with all its rims and threads of gold. A fragrant breath came up from the garden, a hum of soft sound from all the drowsy world out of doors. Agnes, in the corner of the sofa, laying back her head among its pretty cushions, with the smile of fancy on her lips, and the meditative inward light shining in her eyes, playing her foot idly on the carpet, playing her fingers idly among a little knot of flowers which lay at her side, and which, in this sweet indolence, she had not yet taken the trouble to arrange in the little vase—was as complete a picture of maiden meditation—of those charmed fancies, sweet and fearless, which belong to her age and kind, as painter or poet could desire to see.

When Marian suddenly broke in upon the retirement of her sister, disturbed, fluttered, a little afraid, but with no appearance of painfulness, though there was a certain distress in her excitement. Marian's eyes were downcast, abashed, and dewy, her colour unusually bright, her lips apart, her heart beating high. She came into the little quiet room with a sudden burst, as if she had fled from some one; but when she came within the door, paused as suddenly, put up her hands to her face, blushed an overpowering blush, and dropped at once with the shyest, prettiest movement in the world, into a low chair which stood behind the door. Agnes, waking slowly out of her own bright mist of fancy, saw all this with a faint wonder—noticing scarcely anything more than that Marian surely grew prettier every day, and indeed had never looked so beautiful all her life.

"May! you look quite——" lovely, Agnes was about to say; but she paused in consideration of her sister's feelings, and said "frightened" instead.

"Oh, no wonder! Agnes, something has happened," said Marian. She began to look even more frightened as she spoke; yet the pretty saucy lip moved a little into something that resembled suppressed and silent laughter. In spite, however, of this one evidence of a secret mixture of amusement, Marian was extremely grave and visibly afraid.

"What has happened? Is it about Rachel?" asked Agnes, instantly referring Marian's agitation to the subject of her own thoughts.

"About Rachel! you are always thinking about Rachel," said Marian, with a momentary sparkle of indignation. "It is something a great deal more important; it is—oh, Agnes! Sir Langham has been speaking to me——"

Agnes raised herself immediately with a start of eagerness and surprise, accusing herself. She had forgotten all about this close and pressing danger—she had neglected her guardianship—she looked with an appalled and pitying look upon her beautiful sister. In Agnes's eyes, it was perfectly visible already that here was an end of Marian's happiness—that she had bestowed her heart upon Sir Langham, and that accordingly this heart had nothing to do but to break.

"What did he say?" asked Agnes solemnly.

"He said—— oh, I am sure you know very well what he was sure to say," cried Marian, holding down her head, and tying knots in her little handkerchief; "he said—he liked me—and wanted to know if I would consent. But it does not matter what he said," said Marian, sinking her voice very low, and redoubling the knots upon the cambric; "it is not my fault, indeed, Agnes. I did not think he would have done it; I thought it was all like Harry Oswald; and you never said a word. What was I to do?"

"What did *you* say?" asked Agnes again, with breathless anxiety, feeling the reproach, but making no answer to it.

"I said nothing: it was in Mrs Edgerley's morning-room, and she came in almost before he was done speaking; and I was so very glad, and ran away. What could I do?" said again the beautiful culprit, becoming a little more at her ease; but during all this time she never lifted her eyes to her sister's face.

"What *will* you say, then? Marian, you make me very anxious; do not trifle with me," said Agnes.

"It is you who are trifling," retorted the young offender; "for you know if you had told the people at once, as you said you would—but I don't mean to be foolish either," said Marian, rising suddenly, and throwing herself half into her sister's arms; "and now, Agnes, you must go and tell him—indeed you must—and say that we never intended to deceive anybody, and meant no harm."

"*I must tell him!*" said Agnes, with momentary dismay; and then the elder sister put her arm round the beautiful head which leaned on her shoulder, in a caressing and sympathetic tenderness. "Yes, May," said Agnes sadly, "I will do anything you wish—I will say whatever you wish. We ought not to have come here, where you were sure to meet with all these perils. Marian! for my mother's sake you must try to keep up your heart when we get home."

The answer Marian made to this solemn appeal was to raise her eyes, full of wondering and mischievous brightness, and to draw herself immediately from Agnes's embrace with a low laugh of excitement. "Keep up my heart! What do you mean?" said Marian; but she immediately hastened to her own particular sleeping-room, and, lost within its mazy muslin curtains, waited for no explanation. Agnes, disturbed and grave, and much overpowered by her own responsibility, did not know what to think. Present appearances were not much in favour of the breaking of Marian's heart.

CHAPTER VIII
AN EXPLANATION

"But what am I to say?"

To this most difficult question Agnes could not find any satisfactory answer. Marian, though so nearly concerned in it, gave her no assistance whatever. Marian went wandering about the three little rooms, flitting from one to another with unmistakable restlessness, humming inconsistent snatches of song, sometimes a little disposed to cry, sometimes moved to smiles, extremely variable, and full of a sweet and pleasant agitation. Agnes followed her fairy movements with grave eyes, extremely watchful and anxious—was she grieved?—was she pleased? was she really in love?

But Marian made no sign. She would not intrust her sister with any message from herself. She was almost disposed to be out of temper when Agnes questioned her. "You know very well what must be said," said Marian; "you have only to tell him who we are—and I suppose that will be quite enough for Sir Langham. Do you not think so, Agnes?"

"I think it all depends upon how he feels—and how *you* feel," said the anxious sister; but Marian turned away with a smile and made no reply. To tell the truth, she could not at all have explained her own sentiments. She was very considerably flattered by the homage of the handsome guardsman, and fluttered no less by the magnificent and marvellous idea of being a ladyship. There was nothing very much on her part to prevent this beautiful Marian Atheling from becoming as pretty a Lady Portland, and by-and-by, as affectionate a one, as even the delighted imagination of Sir Langham could conceive. But Marian was still entirely fancy free— not at all disinclined to be persuaded into love with Sir Langham, but at present completely innocent of any serious emotions—pleased, excited, in the sweetest flutter of girlish expectation, amusement, and triumph—but nothing more.

And from that corner of the window from which they could gain a sidelong glance at the lawn and partial view of the shrubbery, Sir Langham was now to be descried wandering about as restlessly as Marian, pulling off stray twigs and handfuls of leaves in the most ruthless fashion, and scattering them on his path. Marian drew Agnes suddenly and silently to the window, and pointed out the impatient figure loitering about among the trees. Agnes looked at him with dismay. "Am I to go now—to go out and seek him?—is it proper?" said Agnes, somewhat horrified at the thought. Marian took up the open book from the table, and drew the low chair into the sunshine. "In the evening everybody will be there," said Marian, as she began to read, or to pretend to read. Agnes paused for a moment in the most painful doubt and perplexity. "I suppose, indeed, it had better be done at once," she said to herself, taking up her bonnet with very unenviable feelings. Poor Agnes! her heart beat louder and louder, as she tied the strings with trembling fingers, and prepared to go. There was Marian bending down over the book on her knees, sitting in the sunshine with the full summer light burning upon her hair, and one cheek flushed with the pressure of her supporting hand. She glanced up eagerly, but she said nothing; and Agnes, very pale and extremely doubtful, went upon her strange errand. It was the most perplexing and uncomfortable business in the world—and was it proper? But she reassured herself a little as she went down stairs—if any one should see her going out to seek Sir Langham! "I will tell Mrs Edgerley the reason," thought Agnes—she supposed at least no one could have any difficulty in understanding *that*.

So she hastened along the garden paths, very shyly, looking quite pale, and with a palpitating heart. Sir Langham knew nothing of her approach till he turned round suddenly on hearing the shy hesitating rapid step behind. He thought it was Marian for a moment, and made one eager step forward; then he paused, half expecting, half indignant. Agnes, breathless and hurried, gave him no time to address her—she burst into her little speech with all the eager temerity of fear.

"If you please, Sir Langham, I have something to say to you," said Agnes. "You must have been deceived in us—you do not know who we are. We do not belong to great people—we have never before been in a house like Mrs Edgerley's. I came to tell you at once, for we did not think it honest that you should not know."

"Know—know what?" cried Sir Langham. Never guardsman before was filled with such illimitable amaze.

Agnes had recovered her self-possession to some extent. "I mean, sir," she said earnestly, her face flushing as she spoke, "that we wish you to know who we belong to, and that we are not of your rank, nor like the people here. My father is in the City, and we live at Islington, in Bellevue. We are able to live as we desire to live," said Agnes with a little natural pride, standing very erect, and blushing more deeply than ever, "but we are what people at the Willows would call *poor*."

Her amazed companion stood gazing at her with a blank face of wonder. "Eh?" said Sir Langham. He could not for his life make it out.

"I suppose you do not understand me," said Agnes, who began now to be more at her ease than Sir Langham was, "but what I have said is quite true. My father is an honourable man, whom we have all a right to be proud of, but he has only—only a very little income every year. I meant to have told every one at first, for we did not want to deceive—but there was no opportunity, and whenever Marian told me, we made up our minds that you ought to know. I mean," said Agnes proudly, with a strange momentary impression that she was taller than Sir Langham, who stood before her biting the head of his cane, with a look of the blankest discomfiture—"I mean that we forget altogether what you said to my sister, and understand that you have been deceived."

She was somewhat premature, however, in her contempt. Sir Langham, overpowered with the most complete amazement, had *yet*, at all events, no desire whatever that Marian should forget what he had said to her. "Stop," said the guardsman, with his voice somewhat husky; "do you mean that your father is not a friend of Lord Winterbourne's? He is a squire in Banburyshire—I know all about it—or how could you be here?"

"He is not a squire in Banburyshire; he is in an office in the City— and they asked us here because I had written a book," said Agnes, with a little sadness and great humility. "My father is not a friend of Lord Winterbourne's; but yet I think he knew him long ago."

At these last words Sir Langham brightened a little. "Miss Atheling, I don't want to believe you," said the honest guardsman; "I'll ask Lord Winterbourne."

"Lord Winterbourne knows nothing of us," said Agnes, with an involuntary shudder of dislike; "and now I have told you, Sir Langham, and there is nothing more to say."

As she turned to leave him, the dismayed lover awoke out of his blank astonishment. "Nothing more—not a word—not a message; what did she say?" cried Sir Langham, reddening to his hair, and casting a wistful look at the house where Marian was. He followed her sister with an appealing gesture, yet paused in the midst of it. The unfortunate guardsman had never been in circumstances so utterly perplexing; he could not, would not, give up his love—and yet!

"Marian said nothing—nothing more than I have been obliged to say," said Agnes. She turned away now, and left him with a proud and rapid step, inspired with injured pride and involuntary resentment. Agnes did not quite know what she had expected of Sir Langham, but it surely was something different from this.

CHAPTER IX
AN EXPERIMENT

But there was a wonderful difference between this high-minded and impetuous girl, as she crossed the lawn with a hasty foot, which almost scorned to sink into its velvet softness, and the disturbed and bewildered individual who remained behind her in the bowery path where this interview had taken place. Sir Langham Portland had no very bigoted regard for birth, and no avaricious love of money. He was a very good fellow after his kind, as Sir Langhams go, and would not have done a dishonourable thing, with full knowledge of it, for the three kingdoms; but Sir Langham was a guardsman, a man of fashion, a man of the world; he was not so blinded by passion as to be quite oblivious of what befalls a man who marries a pretty face; he was not wealthy enough or great enough to indulge such a whim with impunity, and the beauty which was enough to elevate a Banburyshire Hall, was not sufficient to gild over the unmentionable enormity of a house in Islington and a father in the City. Fathers in the City who are made of gold may be sufficiently tolerable, but a City papa who was *poor*, and had "only a very small income every year," as Agnes said, was an unimaginable monster, scarcely realisable to the brilliant intellect of Sir Langham. This unfortunate young gentleman wandered about Mrs Edgerley's bit of shrubbery, tearing off leaves and twigs on every side of him, musing much in his perturbed and cloudy understanding, and totally unable to make it out. Let nobody suppose he had given up Marian; that would have made a settlement of the question. But Sir Langham was not disposed to give up his beauty, and not disposed to make a *mésalliance*; and between the terror of losing her and the terror of everybody's sneer and compassion if he gained her, the unhappy lover vibrated painfully, quite unable to come to any decision, or make up his mighty mind one way or the other. He stripped off the leaves of the helpless bushes, but it did him no service; he twisted his mustache, but there was no enlightenment to be gained from that interesting appendage; he collected all his dazzled wits to the consideration of what sort of creature a man might be who was in an office in the City. Finally, a very brilliant and original idea struck upon the heavy intelligence of Sir Langham. He turned briskly out of the byways of the shrubbery, and said to himself with animation, "I'll go and see!"

When Agnes entered again the little dressing-room where her beautiful sister still bent over her book, Marian glanced up at her inquiringly, and finding no information elicited by that, waited a little, then rose, and came shyly to her side. "I only want to know," said Marian, "not because I care; but what did he say?"

"He was surprised," said Agnes proudly, turning her head away; and Agnes would say nothing more, though Marian lingered by her, and tried various hints and measures of persuasion. Agnes was extremely stately, and, as Marian said, "just a little cross," all day. It was rather too bad to be cross, if she was so, to the innocent mischief-maker, who might be the principal sufferer. But Agnes had made up her mind to suffer no talk about Sir Langham; she had quite given him up, and judged him with the most uncompromising harshness. "Yes!" cried Agnes (to herself), with lofty and poetic indignation, "this I suppose is what these fashionable people call love!"

She was wrong, as might have been expected; for that poor honest Sir Langham, galloping through the dusty roads in the blazing heat of an August afternoon, was quite as genuine in this proof of his affection as many a knight of romance. It was quite a serious matter to this poor young man of fashion, before whose tantalised and tortured imagination some small imp of an attendant Cupid perpetually held up the sweetest fancy-portrait of that sweetest of fair faces. This visionary tormentor tugged at his very heart-strings as the white summer dust rose up in a cloud, marking his progress along the whole long line of the Richmond road. He was not going to slay the dragon, the enemy of his princess—that would have been easy work. He was, unfortunate Sir Langham! bound on a despairing enterprise to find out the house which was not a hall in Banburyshire, to make acquaintance, if possible, with the papa who was in the City, and to see "if it would do."

He knew as little, in reality, about the life which Agnes and Marian lived at home, and about their father's house and all its homely economics and quiet happiness, as if he had been a New Zealand chief instead of a guardsman—and galloped along as gravely as if he were going to a funeral, with, all the way, that wicked little imp of a Cupidon tugging at his heart.

Mrs Atheling was alone with her two babies, sighing a little, and full of weariness for the return of the girls; but Susan, better instructed this time, ushered the magnificent visitor into the best room. He stood gazing upon it in blank amazement; upon the haircloth sofa, and the folded leaf of the big old mahogany table in the corner; and the coloured glass candlesticks and flower-vases on the mantel-shelf. Mrs Atheling, who was a little fluttered, and the rosy boy, who clung to her skirts, and, spite of her audible entreaties in the passage, would not suffer her to enter without him, rather increased the consternation of Sir Langham. She was comely; she had a soft voice; a manner quite unpretending and simple, as good in its natural quietness as the highest breeding; yet Sir Langham, at sight of her, heaved from the depths of his capacious bosom a mighty sigh. It would not do; that little wretch of a Cupid, what a wrench it gave him as he tried to cast it out! If it had been a disorderly house or a slatternly mother, Sir Langham might have taken some faint comfort from the thought of rescuing his beautiful Marian from a family unworthy of her; but even to his hazy understanding it became instantly perceptible that this was a home not to be parted with, and a mother much beloved. Marian, a prince might have been glad to marry; but Sir Langham could not screw his fortitude to the pitch of marrying all that little, tidy, well-ordered house in Bellevue.

So he made a great bungle of his visit, and invented a story about being in town on business, and calling to carry the Miss Athelings' messages for home; and made the best he could of so bad a business by a very expeditious retreat. Anything that he did say was about Agnes; and the mother, though a little puzzled and startled by the visit, was content to set it down to the popularity of her young genius. "I suppose he wanted to see what kind of people she belonged to," said Mrs Atheling, with a smile of satisfaction, as she looked round her best room, and drew back with her into the other parlour the rosy little rogues who held on by her gown. She was perfectly correct in her supposition; but, alas! how far astray in the issue of the same.

Sir Langham went to his club—went to the opera—could not rest anywhere, and floundered about like a man bewitched. It would not do—it would not do; but the merciless little Cupid hung on by his heart-strings, and would not be off for all the biddings of the guardsman. He did not return to Richmond; he was heartily ashamed of himself—heartily sick of all the so-called pleasures with which he tried to cheat his disappointment. But Sir Langham had a certain kind of good sense though he was in love, so he applied himself to forgetting "the whole business," and made up his mind finally that it would not do.

The sisters at the Willows, when they found that Sir Langham did not appear that night, and that no one knew anything of him, made their own conclusions on the subject, but did not say a word even to each other. Agnes sat apart silently indignant, and full of a sublime disdain. Marian, with, a deeper colour than usual on her cheek, was, on the contrary, a great deal more animated than was her wont, and attracted everybody's admiration. Had anybody cared to think of the matter, it would have been the elder sister, and not the younger, whom the common imagination could have supposed to have lost a lover; but they went to rest very early that night, and spent no pleasant hour in the pleasant gossip which never failed between them. Sir Langham was not to be spoken of; and Agnes lay awake, wondering what Marian's feelings were, long after Marian, forgetting all about her momentary pique and anger, was fast and sweet asleep.

CHAPTER X
GOING HOME

And now it had come to an end—all the novelty, the splendour, and the excitement of this first visit—and Agnes and Marian were about to go home. They were very much pleased, and yet a little disappointed—glad and eager to return to their mother, yet feeling it would have been something of a compliment to be asked to remain.

Rachel, who was a great deal more vehement and demonstrative than either of them, threw herself into their arms with violent tears. "I have been so happy since ever I knew you," said Rachel—"so happy, I scarcely thought it right when I was not with Louis—and I think I could almost like to be your servant, and go home with you. I could do anything for you."

"Hush!" said Agnes.

"No; it is quite true," cried poor Rachel—"*quite* true. I should like to be your servant, and live with your mother. Oh! I ought to say," she continued, raising herself with a little start and thrill of terror, "that if we were in a different position, and could meet people like equals, I should be so glad—so very glad to be friends."

"But how odd Rachel would think it to live in Bellevue," said Marian, coming to the rescue with a little happy ridicule, which did better than gravity, "and to see no one, even in the street, but the milkman and the greengrocer's boy! for Rachel only thinks of the Willows and Winterbourne; she does not know in the least how things look in Bellevue."

Rachel was beguiled into a laugh—a very unusual indulgence. "When you say that, I think it is a very little cottage like one of the cottages in the village; but you know that is all wrong. Oh, when do you think you will go to Winterbourne?"

"We will write and tell you," said Agnes, "all about it, and how many are going; for I do not suppose Charlie will come, after all; and you will write to us—how often? Every other day?"

Rachel turned very red, then very pale, and looked at them with considerable dismay. "Write!" she said, with a falter in her voice; "I—I never thought of that—I never wrote to any one; I daresay I should do it very badly. Oh no; I shall be sure to find out whenever you come to the Old Wood Lodge."

"But we shall hear nothing of you," said Agnes. "Why should you not write to us? I am sure you do to your brother at home."

"I do *not*," said Rachel, once more drawing herself up, and with flashing eyes. "No one can write letters to us, who have no name."

She was not to be moved from this point; she repeated the same words again and again, though with a very wistful and yielding look in her face. All for Louis! Her companions were obliged to give up the question, after all.

So there was another weeping, sobbing, vehement embrace, and Rachel disappeared without a word into the big bare room down stairs— disappeared to fall again, without a struggle, into her former forlorn life—to yield on her own account, and to struggle with fierce haughtiness for the credit of Louis—leaving the two sisters very thoughtful and compassionate, and full of a sudden eager generous impulse to run away with and take her home.

"Home—to mamma! It would be like heaven to Rachel," said Agnes, in a little enthusiasm, with tears in her eyes.

"Ay, but it would not be like the Willows," said the most practical Marian; and they both looked out with a smile and a sigh upon the beautiful sunshiny lawn, the river in an ecstasy of light and brightness, the little island with all its ruffled willow-leaves, and bethought themselves, finding some amusement in the contrast, of Laurel House, and Myrtle Cottage, and the close secluded walls of Bellevue.

Mrs Atheling had sent the Fly for her daughters—the old Islingtonian fly, with the old white horse, and the coachman with his shiny hat. This vehicle, which had once been a chariot of the gods, looked somewhat shabby as it stood in the broad sunshine before the door of the Willows, accustomed to the fairy coach of Mrs Edgerley. They laughed to themselves very quietly when they caught their first glimpse of it, yet in a momentary weakness were half ashamed; for even Agnes's honest determination to let everybody know their true "rank in life" was not troubled by any fear lest this respectable vehicle should be taken for their own carriage *now*.

"Going, my love?" cried Mrs Edgerley; "the fatal hour—has it really come so soon?—You leave us all *desolée*, of course; how *shall* we exist to-day? And it was so good of you to come. Remember! we shall be dying till we have a new tale from the author of *Hope Hazlewood*. I long to see it. I know it will be charming, or it could not be yours.—And, my love, you look quite lovely—such roses! I think you quite the most exquisite little creature in the world. Remember me to your excellent mamma. Is your carriage waiting? Ah, I am miserable to part with you. Farewell—that dreadful word—farewell!"

Again that light perfumy touch waved over one blushing cheek and then another. Mrs Edgerley continued to wave her hand and make them pretty signals till they reached the door, whither they hastened as quickly and as quietly as possible, not desiring any escort; but few were the privileged people in Mrs Edgerley's morning-room, and no one cared to do the girls so much honour. Outside the house their friend the gardener waited with two bouquets, so rare and beautiful that the timid recipients of the same, making him their humble thanks, scarcely knew how to express sufficient gratitude. Some one was arriving as they departed—some one who, making the discovery of their presence, stalked towards them, almost stumbling over Agnes, who happened to be nearest to him. "Going away?" said a dismayed voice at a considerable altitude. Mr Endicott's thin head positively vibrated with mortification; he stretched it towards Marian, who stood before him smiling over her flowers, and fixed a look of solemn reproach upon her. "I am aware that beauty and youth flee often from the presence of one who looks upon life with a studious eye. This disappointment is not without its object. You are going away?"

"Yes," said Marian, laughing, but with a little charitable compassion for her own particular victim, "and you are just arriving? It is very odd—you should have come yesterday."

"Permit me," said Mr Endicott moodily;—"no; I am satisfied. This experience is well—I am glad to know it. To us, Miss Atheling," said the solemn Yankee, as he gave his valuable assistance to Agnes—"to us this play and sport of fortune is but the proper training. Our business is not to enjoy; we bear these disappointments for the world."

He put them into their humble carriage, and bowed at them solemnly. Poor Mr Endicott! He did not blush, but grew green as he stood looking after the slow equipage ere he turned to the disenchanted Willows. Though he was about to visit people of distinction, the American young gentleman, being in love, did not care to enter upon this new scene of observation and note-making at this moment; so he turned into the road, and walked on in the white cloud of dust raised by the wheels of the fly. The dust itself had a sentiment in it, and belonged to Marian; and Mr Endicott began the painful manufacture of a sonnet, expressing this "experience," on the very spot.

"But *you* ought not to laugh at him, Marian, even though other people do," said Agnes, with superior virtue.

"Why not?" said the saucy beauty; "I laughed at Sir Langham—and I am sure *he* deserved it," she added in an under-tone.

"Marian," said Agnes, "I think—you have named him yourself, or I should not have done it—we had better not say anything about Sir Langham to mamma."

"I do not care at all who names him," said Marian, pouting; but she made no answer to the serious proposition: so it became tacitly agreed between them that nothing was to be said of the superb runaway lover when they got home.

CHAPTER XI
HOME

And now they were at home—the Fly dismissed, the trunks unfastened, and Agnes and Marian sitting with Mamma in the old parlour, as if they had never been away. Yes, they had been away—both of them had come in with a little start and exclamation to this familiar room, which somehow had shrunk out of its proper proportions, and looked strangely dull, dwarfed, and sombre. It was very strange; they had lived here for years, and knew every corner of every chair and every table—and they had only been gone a fortnight—yet what a difference in the well-known room!

"Somebody has been doing something to the house," said Marian involuntarily; and Agnes paused in echoing the sentiment, as she caught a glimpse of a rising cloud on her mother's comely brow.

"Indeed, children, I am grieved to see how soon you have learned to despise your home," said Mrs Atheling; and the good mother reddened, and contracted her forehead. She had watched them with a little jealousy from their first entrance, and they, to tell the truth, had been visibly struck with the smallness and the dulness of the family rooms.

"Despise!" cried Marian, kneeling down, and leaning her beautiful head and her clasped arms upon her mother's knee. "Despise!" said Agnes, putting her arm over Mrs Atheling's shoulder from behind her chair; "oh, mamma, you ought to know better!—we who have learned that there are people in the world who have neither a mother nor a home!"

"Well, then, what is the matter?" said Mrs Atheling; and she began to smooth the beautiful falling hair, which came straying over her old black silk lap, like Danae's shower of gold.

"Nothing at all—only the room is a little smaller, and the carpet a little older than it used to be," said Agnes; "but, mamma, because we notice that, you do not think surely that we are less glad to be at home."

"Well, my dears," said Mrs Atheling, still a little piqued; "your great friend, when he called the other day, did not seem to think there was anything amiss about the house."

"Our great friend!" The girls looked at each other with dismay—who could it be?

"His card is on the mantelpiece," said Mrs Atheling. "He had not very much to say, but he seemed a pleasant young man—Sir Something—Sir Langham; but, indeed, my dear, though, of course, I was pleased to see him, I am not at all sure how far such acquaintances are proper for you."

"He was scarcely *my* acquaintance, mamma," said Agnes, sorrowfully looking down from behind her mother's chair upon Marian, who had hid her face in Mrs Atheling's lap, and made no sign.

"For our rank in life is so different," pursued the prudent mother; "and even though I might have some natural ambition for you, I do not think, Agnes, that it would really be wishing you well to wish that you should form connections so far out of the sphere of your own family as *that*."

"Mamma, it was not me," said Agnes again, softly and under her breath.

"It was no one!" cried Marian, rising up hastily, and suddenly seizing and clipping into an ornamental cross Sir Langham's card, which was upon the mantelpiece. "See, Agnes, it will do to wind silk upon; and nobody cares the least in the world for Sir Langham. Mamma, he used to be like Harry Oswald—that is all—and we were very glad when he went away from the Willows, both Agnes and I."

At this statement, made as it was with a blush and a little confusion, Mrs Atheling herself reddened slightly, and instantly left the subject. It was easy enough to warn her children of the evils of a possible connection with people of superior condition; but when such a thing fluttered really and visibly upon the verge of her horizon, Mrs Atheling was struck dumb. To see her pretty Marian a lady—a baronet's wife—the bride of that superb Sir Langham—it was not in the nature of mortal mother to hear without emotion of such an extraordinary possibility. The ambitious imagination kindled at once in the heart of Mrs Atheling: she held her peace.

And the girls, to tell the truth, were very considerably excited about this visit of Sir Langham's. What did it mean? After a little time they strayed into the best room, and stood together looking at it with feelings by no means satisfactory. The family parlour was the family parlour, and, in spite of all that it lacked, possessed something of home and kindness which was not to be found in all the luxurious apartments of the Willows. But, alas! there was nothing but meagre gentility, blank good order, and unloveliness, in this sacred and reserved apartment, where Bell and Beau never threw the charm of their childhood, nor Mrs Atheling dispersed the kindly clippings of her work-basket. The girls consulted each other with dismayed looks—even

Rachel, if she came, could not stand against the chill of this grim parlour. Marian pulled the poor haircloth sofa into another position, and altered with impatience the stiff mahogany chairs. They scarcely liked to say to each other how entirely changed was their ideal, or how they shrank from the melancholy state of the best room. "Sir Langham was here, Agnes," said Marian; and within her own mind the young beauty almost added, "No wonder he ran away!"

"It is home—it is our own house," said Agnes, getting up for the occasion a little pride.

Marian shrugged her pretty shoulders. "But Susan had better bring any one who calls into the other room."

Yes, the other room, when they returned to it, had brightened again marvellously. Mrs Atheling had put on her new gown, and had a pink ribbon in her cap. As she sat by the window with her work-basket, she was pleasanter to look at than a dozen pictures; and the sweetest Raphael in the world was not so sweet as these two little lovely fairies playing upon the faded old rug at the feet of Mamma. Not all the luxuries and all the prettinesses of Mrs Edgerley's drawingrooms, not even the river lying in the sunshine, and the ruffled silvery willows drooping round their little island, were a fit balance to this dearest little group, the mother and the children, who made beautiful beyond all telling the sombre face of home.

CHAPTER XII
A NEW ERA

It came to be rather an exciting business to Agnes and Marian making their report of what had happened at the Willows—for it was difficult to distract Mamma's attention from Sir Langham, and Papa was almost angrily interested in everything which touched upon Lord Winterbourne. Rachel, of course, was a very prominent figure in their picture; but Mrs Atheling was still extremely doubtful, and questioned much whether it was proper to permit such an acquaintance to her daughters. She was very particular in her inquiries concerning this poor girl—much approved of Rachel's consciousness of her own equivocal position—thought it "a very proper feeling," and received evidence with some solemnity as to her "manners" and "principles." The girls described their friend according to the best of their ability; but as neither of them had any great insight into character, we will not pretend to say that their audience were greatly enlightened,— and extremely doubtful was the mind of Mrs Atheling. "My dear, I might be very sorry for her, but it would not be proper for me to forget you in my sympathy for her," said Mamma, gravely and with dignity. Like so many tender-hearted mothers, Mrs Atheling took great credit to herself for an imaginary severity, and made up her mind that she was proof to the assaults of pity—she who at the bottom was the most credulous of all, when she came to hear a story of distress.

And Papa, who had been moved at once to forbid their acquaintance with children of Lord Winterbourne's, changed his mind, and became very much interested when he heard of Rachel's horror of the supposed relationship. When they came to this part of the story, Mrs Atheling was scandalised, but Papa was full of pity. He said "Poor child!" softly, and with emotion; while Charlie pricked his big ear to listen, though no one was favoured with the sentiments on this subject of the big boy.

"And about the Rector and the old lady who lives at Abingford—papa, why did you never tell us about these people?" said Marian; "for I am sure you must know very well who Aunt Bridget's neighbours were in the Old Wood Lodge."

"I know nothing about the Riverses," said Papa hastily—and Mr Atheling himself, sober-minded man though he was, grew red with an angry glow—"there was a time when I hated the name," he added in an impetuous and rapid undertone, and then he looked up as though he was perfectly aware of the restraining look of caution which his wife immediately turned upon him.

"Such neighbours as are proper for us you will find out when we get there," said Mrs Atheling quietly. "Papa has not been at Winterbourne for twenty years, and we have had too many things to think of since then to remember people whom we scarcely knew."

"Then, I suppose, since papa hated the name once, and Rachel hates it now, they must be a very wicked family," said Marian; "but I hope the Rector is not very bad, for Agnes's sake."

This little piece of malice called for instant explanation, and Marian was very peremptorily checked by father and mother. "A girl may say a foolish thing to other girls," said Mamma, "and I am afraid this Rachel, poor thing, must have been very badly brought up; but you ought to know better than to repeat a piece of nonsense like that."

"When are we to go, mamma?" said Agnes, coming in to cover the blush, half of shame and half of displeasure, with which Marian submitted to this reproof; "it is August now, and soon it will be autumn instead of summer: we shall be going out of town when all the fashionable people go—but I would rather it was May."

"It cannot be May this year," said Mrs Atheling, involuntarily brightening; "but papa is to take a holiday—three weeks; my dears, I do not think I have been so pleased at anything since Bell and Beau."

Since Bell and Beau! what an era that was! And this, too, was a new beginning, perhaps more momentous, though not such a sweet and great revulsion, out of the darkness into the light. Mamma's manner of dating her joys cast them all back into thought and quietness; and Agnes's heart beat high with a secret and mercenary pleasure, exulting like a miser over her hundred and fifty pounds. At this moment, and at many another moment when the young author had clean forgotten *Hope Hazlewood*, the thought came upon her with positive delight of the little hoard in Papa's hands, safely laid up in the office, one whole hundred pounds' worth of family good and gladness still; for she had not the same elevated regard for art as her sister's American admirer—she was not, by any means, in her own estimation, or in anybody else's, a representative woman; and Agnes, who began already to think rather meanly of *Hope Hazlewood*, and press on with the impatience of genius towards a higher excellence, had the greatest satisfaction possible in the earnings of her gentle craft—was it an ignoble delight?

The next morning the two girls, with prudence and caution, began an attack upon the Chancellor of the Exchequer touching the best room. At first Mrs Atheling was entirely horrified at their extravagant ideas. The best room!—what could be desired that was not already attained in that most respectable apartment? but the young rebels held their ground. Mamma put down her work upon her knee, and listened to them quietly. It was not a good sign—she made no interruption as they spoke of mirrors and curtains, carpets and ottomans, couches and easy-chairs: she heard them all to the end with unexampled patience—she only said, "My dears, when you are done I will tell you what I have to say."

What she did say was conclusive upon the subject, though it was met by many remonstrances. "We are going to the Old Wood Lodge," said Mrs Atheling, "and I promise you you shall go into Oxford when we are there, and get some things to make old Aunt Bridget's parlour look a little more like yourselves: but even a hundred pounds, though it is quite a little fortune, will not last for ever—and to furnish *two* rooms! My dears, you do not know any better; but, of course, it is quite ridiculous, and cannot be done."

Thus ended at present their plan for making a little drawing-room out of the best room; for Mamma's judgment, though it was decisive, was reasonable, and they could make no stand against it. They did all they could do under the circumstances; for the first time, and with compunction, they secretly instructed Susan against the long-standing general order of the head of the house. Strangers were no longer to be ushered into the sacred stranger's apartment; but before Susan had any chance of obeying these schismatical orders, Agnes and Marian themselves were falling into their old familiarity with the old walls and the sombre furniture, and were no longer disposed to criticise, especially as all their minds and all their endeavours were at present set upon the family holiday—the conjoint household visit to the country—the glorious prospect of taking possession of the Old Wood Lodge.

In Bellevue, Charlie alone was to be left behind—Charlie, who had not been long enough in Mr Foggo's office to ask for a holiday, and who did not want one very much, if truth must be told; for neither early hours nor late hours told upon the iron constitution of the big boy. When they pitied him who must stay behind, the young gentleman said, "Stuff! Susan, I suppose, can make my coffee as well as any of you," said Charlie; but nobody was offended that he limited the advantages of their society to coffee-making; and even Mrs Atheling, in spite of her motherly anxieties, left her house and her son with comfortable confidence. Harm might happen to the house, Susan being in it, who was by no means so careful as she ought to be of her fire and her candle; but nobody feared any harm to the heir and hope of the house.

CHAPTER XIII
THE OLD WOOD LODGE

And it was late in August, a sultry day, oppressive and thundery, when this little family of travellers made their first entry into the Old Wood Lodge.

It stood upon the verge of a wood, and the side of a hill, looking down into what was not so much a valley as a low amphitheatre, watered by a maze of rivers, and centred in a famous and wonderful old town. The trees behind the little house had burning spots of autumn colour here and there among the masses of green—colour which scarcely bore its due weight and distinction in the tremulous pale atmosphere which waited for the storm; and the leaves cowered and shivered together, and one terrified bird flew wildly in among them, seeking refuge. Under the shadow of three trees stood the low house of two stories, half stone and half timber, with one quaint projecting window in the roof, and a luxuriant little garden round it. But it was impossible to pause, as the new proprietors intended to have done, to note all the external features of their little inheritance. They hurried in, eager to be under shelter before the thunder; and as Mrs Atheling, somewhat timid of it, hurried over the threshold, the first big drops fell heavily among the late roses which covered the front of the house. They were all awed by the coming storm; and they were not acquainted any of them with the louder crash and fiercer blaze of a thunderstorm in the country. They came hastily into Miss Bridget's little parlour, scarcely seeing what like it was, as the ominous still darkness gathered in the sky, and sat down, very silently, in corners, all except Mr Atheling, whose duty it was to be courageous, and who was neither so timid as his wife, nor so sensitive as his daughters. Then came the storm in earnest—wild lightning rending the black sky in sheets and streams of flames—fearful cannonades of thunder, nature's grand forces besieging some rebellious city in the skies. Then gleams of light shone wild and ghastly in all the pallid rivers, and lighted up with an eerie illumination the spires and pinnacles of the picturesque old town; and the succeeding darkness pressed down like a positive weight upon the Old Wood Lodge and its new inmates, who scarcely perceived yet the old furniture of the old sitting-room, or the trim old maid of Miss Bridget Atheling curtsying at the door.

"A strange welcome!" said Papa, hastily retreating from the window, where he had just been met and half blinded by a sudden flash; and Mamma gathered her babies under her wings, and called to the girls to come closer to her, in that one safe corner which was neither near the window, the fireplace, nor the door.

Yes, it was a strange welcome—and the mind of Agnes, imaginative and rapid, threw an eager glance into the future out of that corner of safety and darkness. A thunderstorm, a convulsion of nature! was there any fitness in this beginning? They were as innocent a household as ever came into a countryside; but who could tell what should happen to them there?

Some one else seemed to share the natural thought. "I wonder, mamma, if this is all for us," whispered Marian, half frightened, half jesting. "Are we to make a great revolution in Winterbourne? It looks like it, to see this storm."

But Mrs Atheling, who thought it profane to show any levity during a thunderstorm, checked her pretty daughter with a peremptory "Hush, child!" and drew her babies closer into her arms. Mrs Atheling's thoughts had no leisure to stray to Winterbourne; save for Charlie—and it was not to be supposed that this same thunder threatened Bellevue—all her anxieties were here.

But as the din out of doors calmed down, and even as the girls became accustomed to it, and were able to share in Papa's calculations as to the gradual retreat of the thunder as it rolled farther and farther away, they began to find out and notice the room within which they had crowded. It had only one window, and was somewhat dark, the small panes being over-hung and half obscured by a wild forest of clematis, and sundry stray branches, still bristling with buds, of that pale monthly rose with evergreen leaves, which covered half the front of the house. The fireplace had a rather fantastic grate of clear steel, with bright brass ornaments, so clear and so resplendent as it only could be made by the labour of years, and was filled, instead of a fire, with soft green moss, daintily ornamented with the yellow everlasting flowers. Hannah did not know that these were *immortelles*, and consecrated to the memory of the dead. It was only her rural and old-maidenly fashion of decoration, for the same little rustling posies, dry and unfading, were in the little flower-glasses on the high mantel-shelf, before the little old dark-complexioned mirror, with little black-and-white transparencies set in the slender gilding of its frame, which reflected nothing but a slope of the roof, and one dark portrait hanging as high up as itself upon the opposite wall. It put the room oddly out of proportion, this mirror, attracting the eye to its high strip of light, and deluding the unwary to many a stumble; and Agnes already sat fixedly looking at it, and at the dark and wrinkled portrait reflected from the other wall.

Before the fireplace, where there was no fire, stood a large old-fashioned easy-chair, with no one in it. Are you very sure there is no one in it?—for Papa himself has a certain awe of that strangely-placed seat, which seems to have stood before that same fireplace for many a year. In the twilight, Agnes, if you were alone—you, who of all the family are most inclined to a little visionary superstition, you would find it very hard to keep from trembling, or to persuade yourself that Miss Bridget was not there, where she had spent half a lifetime, sitting in that heavy old easy-chair.

The carpet was a faded but rich and soft old Turkey carpet, the furniture was slender and spider-legged, made of old bright mahogany, as black and as polished as ebony. There was an old cabinet in one corner, with brass rings and ornaments; and in another an old musical instrument, of which the girls were not learned enough to know the precise species, though it belonged to the genus piano. The one small square table in the middle of the room was covered with a table-cover, richly embroidered, but the silk was faded, and the bits of gold were black and dull; and there were other little tables, round and square, with spiral legs and a tripod of feet, one holding a china jar, one a big book, and one a case of stuffed birds. On the whole, the room had somewhat the look of a rather refined and very prim old lady. The things in it were all of a delicate kind and antique fashion. It was not in the slightest degree like these fair and fresh young girls, but on the whole it was a place of which people like those, with a wholesome love of ancestry, had very good occasion to be proud.

And at the door stood Hannah, in a black gown and great white apron, smoothing down the same with her hands, and bobbing a kindly curtsy. Hannah's eyes were running over with delight and anxiety to get at Bell and Beau. She passed over all the rest of the family to yearn over the little ones. "Eh, bless us!" cried Hannah, as, the thunder over, Mrs Atheling began to bestir herself—"children in the house!" It was something almost too ecstatic for her elderly imagination. She volunteered to carry them both up-stairs with the most eager attention. "I ain't so much used to childer," said Hannah, "but, bless ye, ma'am, I love 'um all the same;" and with an instinctive knowledge of this love, Beau condescended to grasp Hannah's spotless white apron, and Bell to mount into her arms. Then the whole family procession went up-stairs to look at the bedrooms—the voices of the girls and the sweet chorus of the babies making the strangest echoes in the lonely house. Hannah acknowledged afterwards, that, half with grief for Miss Bridget, and half for joy of this new life beginning, it would have been a great relief to her to sit down upon the attic stairs and have "a good cry."

CHAPTER XIV
WITHIN AND WITHOUT

The upper floor of the Old Wood Lodge consisted of three rooms; one as large as the parlour down stairs, one smaller, and one, looking to the back, very small indeed. The little one was a lumber-room, and quite unfurnished; the other two were in perfect accordance with the sitting-room. The best bedroom contained a bed of state, with very slender fluted pillars of the same black ebony-like wood, lifting on high a solemn canopy of that ponderous substance called moreen, and still to be found in country inns and seaside lodgings—the colour dark green, with a binding of faded violet. Hangings of the same darkened the low broad lattice window, and chairs of the same were ranged like ghosts along the wall. It was rather a funereal apartment, and the eager investigators were somewhat relieved to find an old-fashioned "tent," with hangings of old chintz, gay with gigantic flowers, in the next room. But the windows!—the broad plain lying low down at their feet, twinkling to the first faint sun-ray which ventured out after the storm—the cluster of spires and towers over which the light brightened and strengthened, striking bold upon the heavy dome which gave a ponderous central point to the landscape, and splintering into a million rays from the pinnacles of Magdalen and St Mary's noble spire, all wet and gleaming with the thunder rain. What a scene it was!—how the passing light kindled all the wan waters, and singled out, for a momentary illumination, one after another of the lesser landmarks of that world unknown. These gazers were not skilled to distinguish between Gothic sham and Gothic real, nor knew much of the distinguishing differences of noble and ignoble architecture. After all, at this distance, it did not much matter—for one by one, as the sunshine found them out, they rose up from the gleaming mist, picturesque and various, like the fairy towers and distant splendours of a morning dream.

"I told you it was pretty, Agnes," said Mr Atheling, who felt himself the exhibitor of the whole scene, and looked on with delight at the success of his private view. Papa, who was to the manner born, felt himself applauded in the admiration of his daughters, and carried Beau upon his shoulder down the creaking narrow staircase, with a certain pride and exultation, calling the reluctant girls to follow him. For lo! upon Miss Bridget's centre table was laid out "such a tea!" as Hannah in all her remembrance had never produced before. Fresh home-made cakes, fresh little pats of butter from the nearest farm—cream! and to crown all, a great china dish full of the last of the strawberries, blushing behind their fresh wet leaves. Hannah, when she had lingered as long as her punctilious good-breeding would permit, and long enough to be very wrathful with Mrs Atheling for intercepting a shower of strawberries from the plates of Bell and Beau, retired to her kitchen slowly, and drawing a chair before the fire, though the evening still was sultry, threw her white apron over her head, and had her deferred and relieving "cry." "Bless you, I'll love 'um all," said Hannah, with a succession of sobs, addressing either herself or some unseen familiar, with whom she was in the habit of holding long conversations. "But it ain't Miss Bridget— that's the truth!"

The ground was wet, the trees were damp, everything had been deluged with the shower of the thunderstorm, and Mrs Atheling did not at all think it prudent that her daughters should go out, though she yielded to them. They went first through the fertile garden, where Marian thought "everything" grew—but were obliged to pause in their researches and somewhat ignorant guesses what everything was, by the unknown charm of that sweet rural atmosphere "after the rain." Though it was very near sunset, the birds were all a-twitter in the neighbouring trees, and everywhere around them rose such a breath of fragrance—open-air fragrance, fresh and cool and sweet, as different from the incense of Mrs Edgerley's conservatory as it was from anything in Bellevue. Running waters trickled somewhere out of sight—it was only the "running of the paths after rain;" and yonder, like a queen, sitting low in a sweet humility, was the silent town, with all its crowning towers. The sunshine, which still lingered on Hannah's projecting window in the roof, had left Oxford half an hour ago—and down over the black dome, the heaven-y-piercing spire and lofty cupola, came soft and grey the shadow of the night.

But behind them, through a thick network of foliage, there were gleams and sparkles of gold, touching tenderly some favourite leaves with a green like the green of spring, and throwing the rest into a shadowy blackness against the half-smothered light. Marian ran into the house to call Hannah, begging her to guide them up into the wood. Agnes, less curious, stood with her hand upon the gate, looking down over this wonderful valley, and wondering if she had not seen it some time in a dream.

"Bless you, miss, if it was to the world's end!" cried Hannah; "but it ain't fit for walking, no more nor a desert; the roads is woeful by Badgeley; look you here!—nought in this wide world but mud and clay."

Marian looked in dismay at the muddy road. "It will not be dry for a week," said the disappointed beauty; "but, Hannah, come here, now that I have got you out, and tell us what every place is—Agnes, here's Hannah—and, if you please, which is the village, and which is the Hall, and where is the Old Wood House?"

"Do you see them white chimneys—and smokes?" said Hannah; "they're a-cooking their dinner just, though tea-time's past—that's the Rector's. But, bless your heart, you ain't likely to see the Hall from here. There's all the park and all the trees atween us and my lord's."

"Do the people like him, Hannah?" asked Agnes abruptly, thinking of her friend.

Hannah paused with a look of alarm. "The people—don't mind nothink about him," said Hannah slowly. "Bless us, miss, you gave me such a turn!"

Agnes looked curiously in the old woman's face, to see what the occasion of this "turn" might be. Marian, paying no such attention, leaned over the low mossy gate, looking in the direction of the Old Wood House. They were quite disposed to enjoy the freedom of the "country," and were neither shawled nor bonneted, though the fresh dewy air began to feel the chill of night. Marian leaned out over the gate, with her little hand thrust up under her hair, looking into the distance with her beautiful smiling eyes. The road which passed this gate was a grassy and almost terraced path, used by very few people, and disappearing abruptly in an angle just after it had passed the Lodge. Suddenly emerging from this angle, with a step which fell noiselessly on the wet grass, meeting the startled gaze of Marian in an instantaneous and ghostlike appearance, came forth what she could see only as, against the light, the figure of a man hastening towards the high-road. He also seemed to start as he perceived the young unknown figures in the garden, but his course was too rapid to permit any interchange of curiosity. Marian did not think he looked at her at all as she withdrew hastily from the gate, and he certainly did not pause an instant in his rapid walk; but as he passed he lifted his hat—a singular gesture of courtesy, addressed to no one, like the salutation of a young king—and disappeared in another moment as suddenly as he came. Agnes, attracted by her sister's low unconscious exclamation, saw him as well as Marian—and saw him as little—for neither knew anything at all of his appearance, save so far as a vague idea of height, rapidity—and the noble small head, for an instant uncovered, impressed their imagination. Both paused with a breathless impulse of respect, and a slight apprehensiveness, till they were sure he must be out of hearing, and then both turned to Hannah, standing in the shadow and the twilight, and growing gradually indistinct all but her white apron, with one unanimous exclamation, "Who is that?"

Hannah smoothed down her apron once more, and made another bob of a curtsy, apparently intended for the stranger. "Miss," said Hannah, gravely, "that's Mr Louis—bless his heart!"

Then the old woman turned and went in, leaving the girls by themselves in the garden. They were a little timid of the great calm and silence; they almost fancied they were "by themselves,"—not in the garden only, but in this whole apparent noiseless world.

CHAPTER XV
THE PARLOUR

And with an excitement which they could not control, the two girls hastened in to the Old Lodge, and to Miss Bridget's dim parlour, where the two candles shed their faint summer-evening light over Mr Atheling reading an old newspaper, and Mamma reclining in the great old easy-chair. The abstracted mirror, as loftily withdrawn from common life as Mr Endicott, refused to give any reflection of these good people sitting far below in their middle-aged and respectable quietness, but owned a momentary vision of Agnes and Marian, as they came in with a little haste and eagerness at the half-open door.

But, after all, to be very much excited, to hasten in to tell one's father and mother, with the heart beating faster than usual against one's breast, and to have one's story calmly received with an "Indeed, my dear!" is rather damping to youthful enthusiasm; and really, to tell the truth, there was nothing at all extraordinary in the fact of Louis passing by a door so near the great house which was his own distasteful home. It was not at all a marvellous circumstance; and as for his salutation, though that was remarkable, and caught their imagination, Marian whispered that she had no doubt it was Louis's "way."

They began, accordingly, to look at the slender row of books in one small open shelf above the little cabinet. The books were in old rich bindings, and were of a kind of reading quite unknown to Agnes and Marian. There were two (odd) volumes of the *Spectator*, *Rasselas*, the Poems of Shenstone, the Sermons of Blair; besides these, a French copy of Thomas-à-Kempis, the *Holy Living and Dying* of Jeremy Taylor, and one of the quaint little books of Sir Thomas Browne. Thrust in hastily beside these ancient and well-attired volumes were two which looked surreptitious, and which were consequently examined with the greatest eagerness. One turned out, somewhat disappointingly, to be a volume of Italian exercises, an old, old school-book, inscribed, in a small, pretty, but somewhat faltering feminine handwriting — handwriting of the last century — with the name of Anastasia Rivers, with a B. A. beneath, which doubtless stood for Bridget Atheling, though it seemed to imply, with a kindly sort of blundering comicality sad enough now, that Anastasia Rivers, though she was no great hand at her exercises, had taken a degree. The other volume was of more immediate interest. It was one of those good and exemplary novels, ameliorated Pamelas, which virtuous old ladies were wont to put into the hands of virtuous young ones, and which was calculated to "instruct as well as to amuse" the unfortunate mind of youth. Marian seized upon this *Fatherless Fanny* with an instant appropriation, and in ten minutes was deep in its endless perplexities. Agnes, who would have been very glad of the novel, languidly took down the *Spectator* instead. Yes, we are obliged to confess—languidly; for, with an excited mind upon a lovely summer night, with all the stars shining without, and only two pale candles within, and Mamma visibly dropping to sleep in the easy-chair—who, we demand, would not prefer, even to Steele and Addison, the mazy mysteries of the Minerva Press?

And Agnes did not get on with her reading; she saw visibly before her eyes Marian skimming with an eager interest the pages of her novel. She heard Papa rustling his newspaper, watched the faint flicker of the candles, and was aware of the very gentle nod by which Mamma gave evidence of the condition of *her* thoughts. Agnes's imagination, never averse to wandering, strayed off into speculations concerning the old lady and her old pupil, and all the life, unknown and unrecorded, which had happed within these quiet walls. Altogether it was somewhat hard to understand the connection between the Athelings and the Riverses—whether some secret of family history lay involved in it, or if it was only the familiar bond formed a generation ago between teacher and child. And this Louis!—his sudden appearance and disappearance—his princely recognition as of new subjects. Agnes made nothing whatever of her *Spectator*—her mind was possessed and restless—and by-and-by, curious, impatient, and a little excited, she left the room with an idea of hastening up-stairs to the chamber window, and looking out upon the night. But the door of the kitchen stood invitingly open, and Hannah, who had been waiting, slightly expectant of some visit, was to be seen within, rising up hastily with old-fashioned respect and a little wistfulness. Agnes, though she was a young lady of literary tastes, and liked to look out upon moon and stars with the vague sentiment of youth, had, notwithstanding, a wholesome relish for gossip, and was more pleased with talk of other people than we are disposed to confess; so she had small hesitation in changing her course and joining Hannah—that homely Hannah bobbing her odd little curtsy, and smoothing down her bright white apron, in the full glow of the kitchen-fire.

The kitchen was indeed the only really bright room in the Old Wood Lodge, having one strip of carpet only on its white and sanded floor, a large deal table, white and spotless, and wooden chairs hard and clear as Hannah's own toil-worn but most kindly hands. There was an old-fashioned settle by the chimney corner, a small bit of looking-glass hanging up by the window, and gleams of ruddy copper, and homely covers of white metal, polished as bright as silver, ornamenting the walls. Hannah wiped a chair which needed no wiping, and set it directly in front of the fire for "Miss," but would not on any account be so "unmannerly" as to sit down herself in the young lady's presence. Agnes wisely contented herself with leaning on the chair, and smiled with a little embarrassment at Hannah's courtesy; it was not at all disagreeable, but it was somewhat different from Susan at home.

"I've been looking at 'um, miss," said Hannah, "sleeping like angels; there ain't no difference that I can see; they look, as nigh as can be, both of an age."

"They are twins," said Agnes, finding out, with a smile, that Hannah's thoughts were taken up, not about Louis and Rachel, but Bell and Beau.

At this information Hannah brightened into positive delight. "Childer's ne'er been in this house," said Hannah, "till this day; and twins is a double blessing. There ain't no more, miss? But bless us all, the time between them darlins and you!"

"We have one brother, besides—and a great many little brothers and sisters in heaven," said Agnes, growing very grave, as they all did when they spoke of the dead.

Hannah drew closer with a sympathetic curiosity. "If that ain't a heart-break, there's none in this world," said Hannah. "Bless their dear hearts, it's best for them. Was it a fever then, miss, or a catching sickness? Dear, dear, it's all one, when they're gone, what it was."

"Hannah, you must never speak of it to mamma," said Agnes; "we used to be so sad—so sad! till God sent Bell and Beau. Do you know Miss Rachel at the Hall? her brother and she are twins too."

"Yes, miss," said Hannah, with a slight curtsy, and becoming at once very laconic.

"And *we* know her," said Agnes, a little confused by the old woman's sudden quietness. "I suppose that was her brother who passed to-night."

"Ay, poor lad!" Hannah's heart seemed once more a little moved. "They say miss is to be a play-actress, and I can't abide her for giving in to it; but Mr Louis, bless him! he ought to be a king."

"You like him, then?" asked Agnes eagerly.

"Ay, poor boy!" Hannah went away hastily to the table, where, in a china basin, in their cool crisp green, lay the homely salads of the garden, about to be arranged for supper. A tray covered with a snow-white cloth, and a small pile of eggs, waited in hospitable preparation for the same meal. Hannah, who had been so long in possession, felt like a humble mistress of the house, exercising the utmost bounties of her hospitality towards her new guests. "Least said's best about them, dear," said Hannah, growing more familiar as she grew a little excited—"but, Lord bless us, it's enough to craze a poor body to see the likes of him, with such a spirit, kept out o' his rights."

"What are his rights, Hannah?" cried Agnes, with new and anxious interest: this threw quite a new light upon the subject.

Hannah turned round a little perplexed. "Tell the truth, I dun know no more nor a baby," said Hannah; "but Miss Bridget, she was well acquaint in all the ways of them, and she ever upheld, when his name was named, that my lord kep' him out of his rights."

"And what did *he* say?" asked Agnes.

"Nay, child," said the old woman, "it ain't no business of mine to tell tales; and Miss Bridget had more sense nor all the men of larning I ever heard tell of. She knew better than to put wickedness into his mind. He's a handsome lad and a kind, is Mr Louis; but I wouldn't be my lord, no, not for all Banburyshire, if I'd done that boy a wrong."

"Then, do you think Lord Winterbourne has *not* done him a wrong?" said Agnes, thoroughly bewildered.

Hannah turned round upon her suddenly, with a handful of herbs and a knife in her other hand. "Miss, he's an unlawful child!" said Hannah, with the most melodramatic effectiveness. Agnes involuntarily drew back a step, and felt the blood rush to her face. When she had delivered herself of this startling whisper, Hannah returned to her homely occupation, talking in an under-tone all the while.

"Ay, poor lad, there's none can mend that," said Hannah; "he's kep' out of his rights, and never a man can help him. If it ain't enough to put him wild, *I* dun know."

"And are you quite sure of that? Does everybody think him a son of Lord Winterbourne's?" said Agnes.

"Well, miss, my lord's not like to own to it—to shame hisself," said Hannah; "but they're none so full of charity at the Hall as to bother with other folkses children. My lord's kep' him since they were babies, and sent the lawyer hisself to fetch him when Mr Louis ran away. Bless you, no; there ain't no doubt about it. Whose son else could he be?"

"But if that was true, he would have no rights. And what did Miss Bridget mean by rights?" asked Agnes, in a very low tone, blushing, and half ashamed to speak of such a subject at all.

Hannah, however, who did not share in all the opinions of respectability, but had a leaning rather, in the servant view of the question, to the pariah of the great old house, took up somewhat sharply this unguarded opinion. "Miss," said Hannah, "you'll not tell me that there ain't no rights belonging Mr Louis. The queen on the throne would be glad of the likes of him for a prince and an heir; and Miss Bridget was well acquaint in all the ways of the Riverses, and was as fine to hear as a printed book: for the matter of that," added Hannah, solemnly, "Miss Taesie, though she would not go through the park-gates to save her life, had a leaning to Mr Louis too."

"And who is Miss Taesie?" said Agnes.

"Miss," said Hannah, in a very grave and reproving tone, "you're little acquaint with our ways; it ain't my business to go into stories—you ask your papa."

"So I will, Hannah; but who is Miss Taesie?" asked Agnes again, with a smile.

Hannah answered only by placing her salad on the tray, and carrying it solemnly to the parlour. Amused and interested, Agnes stood by the kitchen fireside thinking over what she had heard, and smiling as she mused; for Miss Taesie, no doubt, was the Honourable Anastasia Rivers, beneath whose name, in the old exercise-book, stood that odd B. A.

CHAPTER XVI
WINTERBOURNE

The next day the family walked forth in a body, to make acquaintance with the "new neighbourhood." There was Papa and Mamma first of all, Mrs Atheling extremely well dressed, and in all the cheerful excitement of an unaccustomed holiday; and then came Agnes and Marian, pleased and curious—and, wild with delight, little Bell and Beau. Hannah, who was very near as much delighted as the children, stood at the door looking after them as they turned the angle of the grassy path. When they were quite out of sight, Hannah returned to her kitchen with a brisk step, to compound the most delicious of possible puddings for their early dinner. It was worth while now to exercise those half-forgotten gifts of cookery which had been lost upon Miss Bridget; and when everything was ready, Hannah, instead of her black ribbon, put new white bows in her cap. At sight of the young people, and, above all, the children, and in the strange delightful bustle of "a full house," hard-featured Hannah, kind and homely, renewed her youth.

The father and mother sent their children on before them, and made progress slowly, recalling and remembering everything. As for Agnes and Marian, they hastened forward with irregular and fluctuating curiosity— loitering one moment, and running another, but, after their different fashion, taking note of all they saw. And between the vanguard and the rearguard a most unsteady main body, fluttering over the grass like two butterflies, as they ran back and forward from Agnes and Marian to Papa and Mamma "with flichterin' noise and glee," came Bell and Beau. These small people, with handfuls of buttercups and clovertops always running through their rosy little fingers, were to be traced along their devious and uncertain path by the droppings of these humble posies, and were in a state of perfect and unalloyed ecstasy. The little family procession came past the Old Wood House, which was a large white square building, a great deal loftier, larger, and more pretending than their own; in fact, a great house in comparison with their cottage. Round two sides of it appeared the prettiest of trim gardens—a little world of velvet lawn, clipped yews, and glowing flower-beds. The windows were entirely obscured with close Venetian blinds, partially excused by the sunshine, but turning a most jealous and inscrutable blankness to the eyes of the new inhabitants; and close behind the house clustered the trees of the park. As they passed, looking earnestly at the house, some one came out—a very young man, unmistakably clerical, with a stiff white band under his monkish chin, a waistcoat which was very High Church, and the blandest of habitual smiles. He looked at the strangers urbanely, with a half intention of addressing them. The girls were not learned in Church politics, yet they recognised the priestly appearance of the smiling young clergyman; and Agnes, for her part, contemplated him with a secret disappointment and dismay. Mr Rivers himself was said to be High Church. Could this be Mr Rivers? He passed, however, and left them to guess vainly; and Papa and Mamma, whose slow and steady pace threatened every now and then to outstrip these irregular, rapid young footsteps, came up and pressed them onward. "How strange!" Marian exclaimed involuntarily: "if that is he, I am disappointed; but how funny to meet them *both*!"

And then Marian blushed, and laughed aloud, half ashamed to be detected in this evident allusion to Rachel's castles in the air. Her laugh attracted the attention of a countrywoman who just then came out to the door of a little wayside cottage. She made them a little bob of a curtsy, like Hannah's, and asked if they wanted to see the church, "'cause I don't think the gentlemen would mind," said the clerk's wife, the privileged bearer of the ecclesiastical keys; and Mr Atheling, hearing the question, answered over the heads of his daughters, "Yes, certainly they would go." So they all went after her dutifully over the stile, and along a field-path by a rustling growth of wheat, spotted with red poppies, for which Bell and Beau sighed and cried in vain, and came at last to a pretty small church, of the architectural style and period of which this benighted family were most entirely ignorant. Mr Atheling, indeed, had a vague idea that it was "Gothic," but would not have liked to commit himself even to that general principle—for the days of religious architecture and church restorations were all since Mr Atheling's time.

They went in accordingly under a low round-arched doorway, solemn and ponderous, entirely unconscious of the "tressured ornament" which antiquaries came far to see; and, looking with a certain awe at the heavy and solemn arches of the little old Saxon church, were rather more personally attracted, we are pained to confess, by a group of gentlemen within the sacred verge of the chancel, discussing something with solemnity and earnestness, as if it were a question of life and death. Foremost in this group, but occupying, as it seemed, rather an explanatory and apologetic place, and listening with evident anxiety to the deliverance of the others, was a young man of commanding appearance, extremely tall, with a little of the look of ascetic abstraction which belongs to the loftier members of the very high High Church. As the Athelings approached rather timidly under the escort of their humble guide, this gentleman eyed them, with a mixture of observation and haughtiness, as they might have been eyed by the proprietor of the domain. Then he recognised Mr Atheling with such a recognition as the same reigning lord and master might bestow upon an intruder who was only mistaken and not presumptuous. The father of the family rose to the occasion, his colour increased; he drew himself up, and made a formal but really dignified bow to the young clergyman. The little group of advisers did not pause a minute in their discussion; and odd words, which they were not in the habit of hearing, fell upon the ears of Agnes and Marian. "Bad in an archaic point of view—extremely bad; and I never can forgive errors of detail; the best examples are so accessible," said one gentleman. "I do not agree with you. I remember an instance at Amiens," interrupted another. "Amiens, my dear sir!—exactly what I mean to say," cried the first speaker; "behind the date of Winterbourne a couple of hundred years—late work—a debased style. In a church of this period everything ought to be severe."

And accordingly there were severe Apostles in the painted windows— those slender lancet "lights" which at this moment dazzled the eyes of Agnes and Marian; and the new saints in the new little niches were, so far as austerity went, a great deal more correct and true to their "period" than even the old saints, without noses, and sorely worn with weather and irreverence, who were as genuine early English as the stout old walls. But Marian Atheling had no comprehension of this kind of severity. She shrunk away from the altar in its religious gloom—the altar with its tall candlesticks, and its cloth, which was stiff with embroidery—marvelling in her innocent imagination over some vague terror of punishments and penances in a church where "everything ought to be severe." Marian took care to be on the other side of her father and mother, as they passed again the academic group discussing the newly restored sedilia, which was not quite true in point of "detail," and drew a long breath of relief when she was safely outside these dangerous walls. "The Rector! that was the Rector. Oh Agnes!" cried Marian, as Papa announced the dreadful intelligence; and the younger sister, horror-stricken, and with great pity, looked sympathetically in Agnes's face. Agnes herself was moved to look back at the tall central figure, using for a dais the elevation of that chancel. She smiled, but she was a little startled—and the girls went on to the village, and to glance through the trees at the great park surrounding the Hall, with not nearly so much conversation as at the beginning of their enterprise. But it was with a sigh instead of a laugh that Marian repeated, when they went home to dinner and Hannah's magnificent pudding—"So, Agnes, we have seen them both."

CHAPTER XVII
THE CLERGY

Several weeks after this passed very quietly over the Old Wood Lodge and its new inhabitants. They saw "Mr Louis," always a rapid and sudden apparition, pass now and then before their windows, and sometimes received again that slight passing courtesy which nobody could return, as it was addressed to nobody, and only disclosed a certain careless yet courteous knowledge on the part of the young prince that they were there; and they saw the Rector on the quiet country Sabbath-days in his ancient little church, with its old heavy arches, and its new and dainty restorations, "intoning" after the loftiest fashion, and preaching strange little sermons of subdued yet often vehement and impatient eloquence—addresses which came from a caged and fiery spirit, and had no business there. The Winterbourne villagers gaped at his Reverence as he flung his thunderbolts over their heads, and his Reverence came down now and then from a wild uncertain voyage heavenward, down, down, with a sudden dreary plunge, to look at all the blank rustical faces, slumberous or wondering, and chafe himself with fiery attempts to come down to their level, and do his duty to his rural flock. With a certain vague understanding of some great strife and tumult in this dissatisfied and troubled spirit, Agnes Atheling followed him in the sudden outbursts of his natural oratory, and in the painful curb and drawing-up by which he seemed to awake and come to himself. Though she was no student of character, this young genius could not restrain a throb of sympathy for the imprisoned and uncertain intellect beating its wings before her very eyes. Intellect of the very highest order was, without question, errant in that humble pulpit—errant, eager, disquieted—an eagle flying at the sun. The simpler soul of genius vaguely comprehended it, and rose with half-respectful, half-compassionating sympathy, to mark the conflict. The family mother was not half satisfied with these preachings, and greatly lamented that the only church within their reach should be so painfully "high," and so decidedly objectionable. Mrs Atheling's soul was grieved within her at the tall candlesticks, and even the "severe" Apostles in the windows were somewhat appalling to this excellent Protestant. She listened with a certain dignified disapproval to the sermons, not much remarking their special features, but contenting herself with a general censure. Marian too, who did not pretend to be intellectual, wondered a little like the other people, and though she could not resist the excitement of this unusual eloquence, gazed blankly at the preacher after it was over, not at all sure if it was right, and marvelling what he could mean. Agnes alone, who could by no means have told you what he meant—who did not even understand, and certainly could not have explained in words her own interest in the irregular prelection—vaguely followed him nevertheless with an intuitive and unexplainable comprehension. They had never exchanged words, and the lofty and self-absorbed Rector knew nothing of the tenants of the Old Wood Lodge; yet he began to look towards the corner whence that intelligent and watching face flashed upon his maze of vehement and uncertain thought. He began to look, as a relief, for the upward glance of those awed yet pitying eyes, which followed him, yet somehow, in their simplicity, were always before him, steadfastly shining in the calm and deep assurance of a higher world than his. It was not by any means, at this moment, a young man and a young woman looking at each other with the mutual sympathy and mutual difference of nature; it was Genius, sweet, human, and universal, tender in the dews of youth—and Intellect, nervous, fiery, impatient, straining like a Hercules after the Divine gift, which came to the other sleeping, as God gives it to His beloved.

The Curate of Winterbourne was the most admirable foil to his reverend principal. This young and fervent churchman would gladly have sat in the lower seat of the restored sedilia, stone-cold and cushionless, at any risk of rheumatism, had not his reverence the Rector put a decided interdict upon so extreme an example of rigid Anglicanism. As it was, his bland and satisfied youthful face in the reading-desk made the strangest contrast in the world to that dark, impetuous, and troubled countenance, lowering in handsome gloom from the pulpit. The common people, who held the Rector in awe, took comfort in the presence of the Curate, who knew all the names of all the children, and was rather pleased than troubled when they made so bold as to speak to him about a place for Sally, or a 'prenticeship for John. His own proper place in the world had fallen happily to this urbane and satisfied young gentleman. He was a parish priest born and intended, and accordingly there was not a better parish priest in all Banburyshire than the Reverend Eustace Mead. While the Rector only played and fretted over these pretty toys of revived Anglicanism, with which he was not able to occupy his rapid and impetuous intellect, they sufficed to make a pleasant reserve of interest in the life of the Curate, who was by no means an impersonation of intellect, though he had an acute and practical little mind of his own, much more at his command than the mind of Mr Rivers was at his. And the Curate preached devout little sermons, which the rustical people did not gape at; while the Rector, out of all question, and to the perception of everybody, was, in the most emphatic sense of the words, the wrong man in the wrong place.

So far as time had yet gone, the only intercourse with their neighbours held by the Athelings was at church, and their nearest neighbours were those clerical people who occupied the Old Wood House. Mr Rivers was said to have a sister living with him, but she was "a great invalid," and never visible; and on no occasion, since his new parishioners arrived, had the close Venetian blinds been raised, or the house opened its eyes. There it stood in the sunshine, in that most verdant of trim old gardens, which no one ever walked in, nor, according to appearances, ever saw, with its three rows of closed windows, blankly green, secluded and forbidding, which no one within ever seemed tempted to open to the sweetest of morning breezes, or the fragrant coolness of the night. Agnes, taking the privilege of her craft, was much disposed to suspect some wonderful secret or mystery in this monkish and ascetic habitation; but it was not difficult to guess the secret of the Rector, and there was not a morsel of mystery in the bland countenance of smiling Mr Mead.

By this time Mrs Atheling and her children were alone. Papa had exhausted his holiday, and with a mixture of pleasure and unwillingness returned to his office duties; and Mamma, though she had so much enjoyment of the country, which was "so good for the children," began to sigh a little for her other household, to marvel much how Susan used her supremacy, and to be seized with great compunctions now and then as to the cruelty "of leaving your father and Charlie by themselves so long." The only thing which really reconciled the good wife to this desertion, was the fact that Charlie himself, without any solicitation, and in fact rather against his will, was to have a week's holiday at Michaelmas, and of course looked forward in his turn to the Old Wood Lodge. Mrs Atheling had made up her mind to return with her son, and was at present in a state of considerable doubt and perplexity touching Agnes and Marian, Bell and Beau. The roses on the cheeks of the little people had blossomed so sweetly since they came to the country, Mrs Atheling almost thought she could trust her darlings to Hannah, and that "another month would do them no harm."

CHAPTER XVIII
A NEW FRIEND

September had begun, but my lord and his expected guests had not yet arrived at the Hall. Much talk and great preparations were reported in the village, and came in little rivulets of intelligence, through Hannah and the humble merchants at the place, to the Old Wood Lodge; but Agnes and Marian, who had not contrived to write to her, knew nothing whatever of Rachel, and vainly peeped in at the great gates of the park, early and late, for the small rapid figure which had made so great an impression upon their youthful fancy. Then came the question, should they speak to Louis, who was to be seen sometimes with a gun and a gamekeeper, deep in the gorse and ferns of Badgeley Wood. Hannah said this act of rebellious freedom had been met by a threat on the part of my lord to "have him up" for poaching, which threat only quickened the haughty boy in his love of sport. "You may say what you like, children, but it is very wrong and very sinful," said Mrs Atheling, shaking her head with serious disapproval, "and especially if he brings in some poor gamekeeper, and risks his children's bread;" and Mamma was scarcely to be satisfied with Hannah's voluble and eager disclaimer—Mr Louis would put no man in peril. This excellent mother held her prejudices almost as firmly as her principles, and compassionately added that it was no wonder—poor boy, considering—for she could not understand how Louis could be virtuous and illegitimate, and stood out with a repugnance, scarcely to be overcome, against any friendship between her own children and these unfortunate orphans at the Hall.

One of these bright afternoons, the girls were in the garden discussing eagerly this difficult question; for it would be very sad to bring Rachel to the house, full of kind and warm expectations, and find her met by the averted looks of Mamma. Her two daughters, however, though they were grieved, did not find it at all in their way to criticise the opinions of their mother; they concerted little loving attacks against them, but thought of nothing more.

And these two found great occupation in the garden, where Bell and Beau played all the day long, and which Mrs Atheling commanded as she sat by the parlour window with her work-basket. This afternoon the family group was fated to interruption. One of the vehicles ascending the high-road, which was not far from the house, drew up suddenly at sight of these young figures in old Miss Bridget's garden. Even at this distance a rather rough and very peremptory voice was audible ordering the groom, and then a singular-looking personage appeared on the grassy path. This was a very tall woman, dressed in an old-fashioned brown cloth pelisse and tippet, with an odd bonnet on her head which seemed an original design, contrived for mere comfort, and owning no fashion at all. She was not young certainly, but she was not so old either, as the archæological "detail" of her costume might have warranted a stranger in supposing. Fifty at the very utmost, perhaps only forty-five, with a fresh cheek, a bright eye, and all the demeanour of a country gentleman, this lady advanced upon the curious and timid girls. That her errand was with them was sufficiently apparent from the moment they saw her, and they stood together very conscious, under the steady gaze of their approaching visitor, continuing to occupy themselves a little with the children, yet scarcely able to turn from this unknown friend. She came along steadily, without a pause, holding still in her hand the small riding-whip which had been the sceptre of her sway over the two stout grey ponies waiting in the high-road—came along steadily to the door, pushed open the gate, entered upon them without either compliment or salutation, and only, when she was close upon the girls, paused for an instant to make the *brusque* and sudden inquiry, "Well, young people, who are you?"

They did not answer for the moment, being surprised in no small degree by such a question; upon which the stranger repeated it rather more peremptorily. "We are called Atheling," said Agnes, with a mixture of pride and amusement. The lady laid her hand heavily upon the girl's shoulder, and turned her half round to the light. "What relation?" said this singular inquisitor; but while she spoke, there became evident a little moistening and relaxation of her heavy grey eyelid, as if it was with a certain emotion she recalled the old owner of the old lodge, whom she did not name.

"My father was Miss Bridget's nephew; she left the house to him," said Agnes; and Marian too drew near in wondering regard and sympathy, as two big drops, like the thunder-rain, fell suddenly and quietly over this old lady's cheeks.

"So! you are Will Atheling's daughters," said their visitor, a little more roughly than before, as if from some shame of her emotion; "and that is your mother at the window. Where's Hannah? for I suppose you don't know me."

"No," said Agnes, feeling rather guilty; it seemed very evident that this lady was a person universally known.

"Will Atheling married—married—whom did he marry?" said the visitor, making her way to the house, and followed by the girls. "Eh! don't you know, children, what was your mother's name? Franklin? yes, to be sure, I remember her a timid pretty sort of creature; ah! just like Will."

By this time they were at the door of the parlour, which she opened with an unhesitating hand. Mrs Atheling, who had seen her from the window, was evidently prepared to receive the stranger, and stood up to greet her with a little colour rising on her cheek, and, as the girls were astonished to perceive, water in her eyes.

This abrupt and big intruder into the family room showed more courtesy to the mother than she had done to the girls; she made a sudden curtsy, which expression of respect seemed to fill up all the requirements of politeness in her eyes, and addressed Mrs Atheling at once, without any prelude. "Do you remember me?"

"I think so—Miss Rivers?" said Mrs Atheling with considerable nervousness.

"Just so—Anastasia Rivers—once not any older than yourself. So—so— and here are you and all your children in my old professor's room."

"We have made no change in it; everything is left as it was," said Mrs Atheling.

"The more's the pity," answered the abrupt and unscrupulous caller. "Why, it's not like *them*—not a bit; as well dress them in her old gowns, dear old soul! Ay well, it was a long life—no excuse for grieving; but at the last, you see, at the last, it's come to its end."

"We did not see her," said Mrs Atheling, with an implied apology for "want of feeling," "for more than twenty years. Some one, for some reason, we cannot tell what, prejudiced her mind against William and me."

"Some one!" said Miss Rivers, with an emphatic toss of her head. "You don't know of course who it was. *I* do: do you wish me to tell you?"

Mrs Atheling made no answer. She looked down with some confusion, and began to trifle with the work which all this time had lain idly on her knee.

"If there's any ill turn he can do you now," said Miss Rivers pointedly, "he will not miss the chance, take my word for it; and in case he tries it, let me know. Will Atheling and I are old friends, and I like the look of the children. Good girls, are they? And is this all your family?"

"All I have alive but one boy," said Mrs Atheling.

"Ah!" said her visitor, looking up quickly. "Lost some?—never mind, child, you'll find them again; and here am I, in earth and heaven a dry tree!"

After a moment's pause she began to speak again, in an entirely different tone. "These young ones must come to see me," said their new friend—"I like the look of them. You are very pretty, my dear, you are quite as good as a picture; but I like your sister just as well as you. Come here, child. Have you had a good education? Are you clever? Nonsense! Why do you blush? People can't have brains without knowing of it. Are you clever, I say?"

"I don't think so," said Agnes, unable to restrain a smile; "but mamma does, and so does Marian." Here she came to an abrupt conclusion, blushing at herself. Miss Rivers rose up from her seat, and stood before her, looking down into the shy eyes of the young genius with all the penetrating steadiness of her own.

"I like an honest girl," said the Honourable Anastasia, patting Agnes's shoulder rather heavily with her strong hand. "Marian—is she called Marian? That's not an Atheling name. Why didn't you call her Bride?"

"She is named for me," said Mrs Atheling with some dignity. And then she added, faltering, "We had a Bridget too; but——"

"Never mind," said Miss Rivers, lifting her hand quickly—"never mind, you'll find them again. She's very pretty—prettier than any one I know about Banburyshire; but for heaven's sake, child, mind what you're about, and don't let any one put nonsense in your head. Your mother could tell you what comes of such folly, and so could I. By the by, children, you are much of an age. Do you know anything of those poor children at the Hall?"

"We know Rachel," said Agnes eagerly. "We met her at Richmond, and were very fond of her; and I suppose she is coming here."

"Rachel!" said Miss Rivers, with a little contempt. "I mean the boy. Has Will Atheling seen the boy?"

"My husband met him once when he came here first," said Mrs Atheling; "and he fancied—fancied—imagined—he was like——"

"My father!" The words were uttered with an earnestness and energy which brought a deep colour over those unyouthful cheeks. "Yes, to be sure—every one says the same. I'd give half my fortune to know the true story of that boy!"

"Rachel says," interposed Agnes, eagerly taking advantage of anything which could be of service to her friend, "that Louis will not believe that they belong to Lord Winterbourne."

The eyes of the Honourable Anastasia flashed positive lightning; then a shadow came over her face. "That's nothing," she said abruptly. "No one who could help it would be content to belong to *him*. Now, I'll send some day for the children: send them over to see me, will you? Ah, where's Hannah—does she suit you? She was very good to *her*, dear old soul!"

"And she is very good to the children," said Mrs Atheling, as she followed her visitor punctiliously to the door. When they reached it, Miss Rivers turned suddenly round upon her—

"You are not rich, are you? Don't be offended; but, if you are able, change all this. I'm glad to see you in the house; but this, you know, *this* is like her gowns and her turbans—make a change."

Here Hannah appeared from her kitchen, curtsying deeply to Miss Taesie, who held a conversation with her at the gate; and finally went away, with her steady step and her riding-whip, having first plucked one of the late pale roses from the wall. Mrs Atheling came in with a degree of agitation not at all usual to the family mother. "The first time I ever saw her," said Mrs Atheling, "when I was a young girl newly married, and she a proud young beauty just on the eve of the same. I remember her, in her hat and her riding-habit, pulling a rose from Aunt Bridget's porch—and there it is again."

"Ma'am," said Hannah, coming in to spread the table, "Miss Taesie never comes here, late or early, but she gathers a rose."

CHAPTER XIX
GOSSIP

"But, mamma, if she was just on the eve of the same, why is she only Miss Rivers now?" asked Marian, very curious on this subject of betrothments and marriages.

"It is a very long story, my dear," said Mrs Atheling. As a general principle, Mamma was not understood to have any special aversion to long stories, but she certainly showed no inclination whatever to enter into this.

"So much the better if you will tell it, mamma," said Agnes; and they came close to her, with their pretty bits of needlework, and their looks of interest; it was not in the heart of woman to refuse.

"Well, my dears," said Mrs Atheling, with a little reluctance, "somehow we seem to be brought into the very midst of it again, though we have scarcely heard their names for twenty years. This lady, though she is almost as old as he is, is niece to Lord Winterbourne. The old lord was only his stepbrother, and a great deal older than he—and Miss Anastasia was the only child of the old lord. You may suppose how disappointed he was, with all his great estates entailed, and the title—and nothing but a daughter; and everybody said, when the old lady died, that he would marry again."

"*Did* he marry again?" said Marian, as Mamma came to a sudden and unexpected pause.

"No, my dear; for then trouble came," said Mrs Atheling. "Miss Anastasia was a beautiful young lady, always very proud, and very wise and sensible, but a great beauty for all that; and she was to be married to a young gentleman, a baronet and a very great man, out of Warwickshire. The present lord was then the Honourable Reginald Rivers, and dreadful wild. Somehow, I cannot tell how it was, he and Sir Frederick quarrelled, and then they fought; and after his wound that fine young gentleman fell into a wasting and a consumption, and died at twenty-five; and that is the reason why Miss Anastasia has never been married, and I am afraid, though it is so very wrong to say so, *hates* Lord Winterbourne."

"Oh, mamma! I am sure I should, if I had been like her!" cried Marian, almost moved to tears.

"No, my darling, not to hate him," said Mrs Atheling, shaking her head, "or you would forget all you have been taught since you were a child."

"I do not understand him, mamma," said Agnes: "does everybody hate him—has he done wrong to every one?"

Mrs Atheling sighed. "My dears, if I tell you, you must forget it again, and never mention it to any one. Papa had a pretty young sister, little Bride, as they all called her, the sweetest girl I ever saw. Mr Reginald come courting her a long time, but at last she found out—oh girls! oh, children!—that what he meant was not true love, but something that it would be a shame and a sin so much as to name; and it broke her dear heart, and she died. Her grave is at Winterbourne; that was what papa and I went to see the first day."

"Mamma," cried Agnes, starting up in great excitement and agitation, "why did you suffer us to know any one belonging to such a man?"

"Well, my dear," said Mrs Atheling, a little discomposed by this appeal. "I thought it was for the best. Coming here, we were sure to be thrown into their way—and perhaps he may have repented. And then Mrs Edgerley was very kind to you, and I did not think it right, for the father's sake, to judge harshly of the child."

Marian, who had covered her face with her hands, looked up now with abashed and glistening eyes. "Is that why papa dislikes him so?" said Marian, very low, and still sheltering with her raised hands her dismayed and blushing face.

Mrs Atheling hesitated a moment. "Yes," she said doubtfully, after a pause of consideration—"yes; that and other things."

But the inquiry of the girls could not elicit from Mamma what were the other things which were sufficient to share with this as motives of Mr Atheling's dislike. They were inexpressibly shocked and troubled by the story, as people are who, contemplating evil at a visionary distance, and having only a visionary belief in it, suddenly find a visible gulf yawning at their own feet; and Agnes could not help thinking, with horror and disgust, of being in the same room with this man of guilt, and of that polluting kiss of his, from which Rachel shrank as from the touch of pestilence. "Such a man ought to be marked and singled out," cried Agnes, with unreasoning youthful eloquence: "no one should dare to bring him into the same atmosphere with pure-minded people; everybody ought to be warned of who and what he was."

"Nay; God has not done so," said Mrs Atheling with a sigh. "He has offended God more than he ever could offend man, but God bears with him. I often say so to your father when we speak of the past. Ought we, who are so sinful ourselves, to have less patience than God?"

After this the girls were very silent, saying nothing, and much absorbed with their own thoughts. Marian, who perhaps for the moment found a certain analogy between her father's pretty sister and herself, was wrapt in breathless horror of the whole catastrophe. Her mind glanced back upon Sir Langham—her fancy started forward into the future; but though the young beauty for the moment was greatly appalled and startled, she could not believe in the possibility of anything at all like this "happening to me!" Agnes, for her part, took quite a different view of the matter. The first suggestion of her eager fancy was, what could be done for Louis and Rachel, to deliver them from the presence and control of such a man? Innocently and instinctively her thoughts turned upon her own gift, and the certain modest amount of power it gave her. Louis might get a situation like Charlie, and be helped until he was able for the full weight of his own life; and Rachel, another sister, could come home to Bellevue. So Agnes, who at this present moment was writing in little bits, much interrupted and broken in upon, her second story, rose into a delightful anticipatory triumph, not of its fame or success, though these things did glance laughingly across her innocent imagination, but of its mere ignoble coined recompense, and of all the great things for these two poor orphans which might be done in Bellevue.

And while the mother and the daughters sat at work in the shady little parlour, where the sunshine did not enter, but where a sidelong reflection of one waving bough of clematis, dusty with blossom, waved across the little sloping mirror, high on the wall, Hannah sat outside the open door, watching with visible delight, and sometimes joining for an instant with awkward kindliness, the sports of Bell and Beau. They rolled about on the soft grass, ran about on the garden paths, tumbled over each other and over everything in their way, but, with the happy immunity of children in the country, "took no harm." Hannah had some work in her great white apron, but did not so much as look at it. She had no eye for a rare passenger upon the grassy byway, and scarcely heard the salutation of the Rector's man. All Hannah's soul and thoughts were wrapt up in the "blessed babies," who made her old life blossom and rejoice; and it was without any intervention of their generally punctilious attendant that a light and rapid step came gliding over the threshold of the Lodge, and a quiet little knock sounded lightly on the parlour door. "May I come in, please?" said a voice which seemed to Agnes to be speaking out of her dream; and Mrs Atheling had not time to buckle on her armour of objection when the door opened, and the same little light rapid figure came bounding into the arms of her daughters. Once there, it was not very difficult to reach to the good mother's kindly heart.

CHAPTER XX
RACHEL

"Yes, I only came to-day," said Rachel, who kept her eyes wistfully upon Mrs Atheling, though she spoke to Agnes. "They made me go to town after you left, and then kept me *so* long at the Willows. Next season they say I am to come out, and somebody has offered me an engagement; but indeed, indeed," cried Rachel, suddenly firing with one of her outbursts of unexpected energy, "I never will!"

The girls scarcely knew what answer to make in presence of their mother. They had not been trained to have independent friendships, and now waited anxiously, turning silent looks of appeal upon Mamma. Mamma all at once had become exceedingly industrious, and neither looked up nor spoke.

"But then you might live in London, perhaps, instead of here; and I should be very glad if you were near us," said Agnes, with a good deal of timidity. Agnes, indeed, was not thinking what she said—her whole attention wandered to her mother.

"I do not mind for myself," said Rachel, with a deep sigh. "I do not think I should care if there were a hundred people to hear me sing, instead of a dozen, for I know very well not one of them would care anything for *me*; but I have to remember Louis. I cannot disgrace Louis. It is bad enough for him as it is, without adding any more."

Again there was a pause. Rachel's poor little palpitating heart beat very loud and very high. "I thought I should be welcome when I came here," she said, freezing half into her unnatural haughtiness, and half with an unconscious and pitiful tone of appeal; "but I never intruded upon any one—never! and if you do not wish me to be here, I can go away."

She turned to go away as she spoke, her little figure rising and swelling with great subdued emotion; but Mrs Atheling immediately rose and stretched out her hand to detain her. "Do not go away, my dear; the girls are very fond of you," said Mrs Atheling; and it cost this good mother, with her ideas of propriety, a very considerable struggle with herself to say these simple words.

Rachel stood before her a moment irresolute and uncertain, not appearing even to hear what Agnes and Marian, assured by this encouragement, hastened to say. The contest was violent while it lasted between Louis's sister, who was his representative, and the natural little humble child Rachel, who had no pride, and only wanted the kindly succour of love; but at last nature won the day. She seized upon Mrs Atheling's hand hastily and kissed it, with a pretty appealing gesture. "They do everything you tell them," cried Rachel suddenly. "I never had any mother—never even when we were babies. Oh, will you tell me sometimes what I ought to do?"

It was said afterwards in the family that at this appeal Mamma, fairly vanquished and overcome, "almost cried;" and certain it was that Rachel immediately took possession of the stool beside her, and remained there not only during this visit, but on every after occasion when she came. She brightened immediately into all her old anxious communicativeness, concealing nothing, but pouring out her whole heart.

"Louis told me he had seen you in the garden," said Rachel, with a low laugh of pleasure; "but when I asked which it was, he said he knew nothing of Agnes and Marian, but only he had seen a vision looking over the old gate. I never know what Louis means when he speaks nonsense," said Rachel, with an unusual brightness; "and I am so glad. I never heard him speak so much nonsense since we came to the Hall."

"And are you left in the Hall all by yourselves, two young creatures?" asked Mrs Atheling, with curiosity. "It must be very melancholy for you."

"Not to be alone!" cried Rachel. "But very soon my lord is coming, with a great household of people; and then—I almost faint when I think upon it. What shall I do?"

"But, Rachel, Mrs Edgerley is very kind to you," said Agnes.

Rachel answered after her usual fashion: "I do not care at all for myself—it is nothing to me; but Louis—oh, Louis!—if he is ever seen, the people stare at him as they would at a horse or a hound; and Lord Winterbourne tries to have an opportunity to speak and order him away, and when he shoots, he says he will put him in prison. And then Louis knows when they send for me, and sometimes stands under the window and hears me singing, and is white with rage to hear; and then he says he cannot bear it, and must go away, and then I go down upon my knees to him. I know how it will happen—everything, everything! It makes him mad to have to bear it. Oh, I wish I knew anything that I could do!"

"Mamma," said Agnes earnestly, "Rachel used to tell us all this at the Willows. Do you not think he ought to go away?"

Mrs Atheling shook her head in perplexity; and instead of answering, asked a question, "Does he not think it his duty, my dear, to obey your—your father?" said Mamma doubtfully.

"But he is not our father—oh no, no, indeed he is not! I should know he was not, even without Louis," cried Rachel, unaware what a violent affirmation this was. "Louis says we could not have any father who would not be a disgrace to us, being as we are—and Louis must be right; but even though he might be a bad man, he could not be like Lord Winterbourne. He takes pleasure in humiliating us—he never cared for us all our life."

There was something very touching in this entire identification of these two solitary existences which still were but one life; and Rachel was not Rachel till she came to the very last words. Before that, with the strange and constantly varying doubleness of her sisterly character, she had been once again the representative of Louis. One thing struck them all as they looked at her small features, fired with this sudden inspiration of Louis's pride and spirit. About as different as possible—at the extreme antipodes of unresemblance—were their two visitors of this day,—this small little fairy, nervous, timid, and doubtful, fatherless, homeless, and without so much as a name, and that assured and commanding old lady, owning no superior, and as secure of her own position and authority as any reigning monarch. Yes, they were about as dissimilar as two human creatures could be; yet the lookers-on were startled to recognise that subtle link of likeness, seldom a likeness of features, which people call family resemblance. Could it have come through this man, who was so repugnant to them both?

"They are all coming down on Monday next week," said Rachel, "so we have just three days all to ourselves; and I thought, perhaps—perhaps, if you please to let me, I might bring Louis to-night?"

"Surely, my dear," said Mrs Atheling.

"Oh, thank you!—thank you very much!" cried Rachel, once more bestowing an eager yet shy caress upon that motherly hand. "Louis is not like me at all," added the anxious sister, afraid lest he should suffer by any preconceived notion of resemblance. "He is a man; and old Miss Bridget used to call him a noble brave boy, like what you read of in books. I do not know," said Rachel, "I never read of any one, even in a book, like Louis. I think he ought to be a king."

"But, indeed, Rachel," said Agnes, "I am quite sure you are wrong. Ask mamma. You ought to let him go away."

"Do *you* think so?" said Rachel wistfully, looking up in Mrs Atheling's face.

But Mrs Atheling, though under any other circumstances she would of course have insisted upon the absolute propriety of a young man "making his own way," paused, much perplexed, and answered nothing for the moment. "My dears," she said at last, very doubtfully, "I do not know at all what to say. You should have some one who could advise you better; and it depends on the young gentleman's inclinations, and a great many things beside that I am not able to judge of; for, indeed, though it may only be my old-fashioned notions, I do not like to hear of young people going against the advice of their friends."

CHAPTER XXI
THE YOUNG PRINCE

It may be supposed that, after all they had heard of him, the Athelings prepared themselves with a little excitement for the visit of Louis. Even Mrs Atheling, who disapproved of him, could not prevent herself from wandering astray in long speculations about the old lord—and it seemed less improper to wonder and inquire concerning a boy, whom the Honourable Anastasia herself inquired after and wondered at. As for the girls, Louis had come to be an ideal hero to both of them. The adored and wonderful brother of Rachel—though Rachel was only a girl, and scarcely so wise as themselves—the admiration of Miss Bridget, and the anxiety of Miss Anastasia, though these were only a couple of old ladies, united in a half deification of the lordly young stranger, whose own appearance and manner were enough to have awakened a certain romantic interest in their simple young hearts. They were extremely concerned to-night about their homely tea-table—that everything should look its best and brightest; and even contrived, unknown to Hannah, to filch and convert into a temporary cake-basket that small rich old silver salver, which had been wont to stand upon one of Miss Bridget's little tables for cards. Then they robbed the garden for a sufficient bouquet of flowers; and then Agnes, half against her sister's will, wove in one of those pale roses to Marian's beautiful hair. Marian, though she made a laughing protest against this, and pretended to be totally indifferent to the important question, which dress she should wear? clearly recognised herself as the heroine of the evening. *She* knew very well, if no one else did, what was the vision which Louis had seen at the old gate, and came down to Miss Bridget's prim old parlour in her pretty light muslin dress with the rose in her hair, looking, in her little flutter and palpitation, as sweet a "vision of delight" as ever appeared to the eyes of man.

And Louis came—came—condescended to take tea—stayed some two hours or so, and then took his departure, hurriedly promising to come back for his sister. This much-anticipated hero—could it be possible that his going away was the greatest relief to them all, and that no one of the little party felt at all comfortable or at ease till he was gone? It was most strange and deplorable, yet it was most true beyond the possibility of question; for Louis, with all a young man's sensitive pride stung into bitterness by his position, haughtily repelled the interest and kindness of all these women. He was angry at Rachel—poor little anxious timid Rachel, who almost looked happy when they crossed this kindly threshold—for supposing these friends of hers, who were all women, could be companions for him; he was angry at himself for his anger; he was in the haughtiest and darkest frame of his naturally impetuous temper, rather disposed to receive as an insult any overture of friendship, and fiercely to plume himself upon his separated and orphaned state. They were all entirely discomfited and taken aback by their stately visitor, whom they had been disposed to receive with the warmest cordiality, and treat as one whom it was in their power to be kind to. Though his sister did so much violence to her natural feelings that she might hold her ground as his representative, Louis did not by any means acknowledge her deputyship. In entire opposition to her earnest and anxious frankness, Louis closed himself up with a jealous and repellant reserve; said nothing he could help saying, and speaking, when he did speak, with a cold and indifferent dignity; did not so much as refer to the Hall or Lord Winterbourne, and checked Rachel, when she was about to do so, with an almost imperceptible gesture, peremptory and full of displeasure. Poor Rachel, constantly referring to him with her eyes, and feeling the ground entirely taken from beneath her feet, sat pale and anxious, full of apprehension and dismay. Marian, who was not accustomed to see her own pretty self treated with such absolute unconcern, took down *Fatherless Fanny* from the bookshelf, and played with it, half reading, half "pretending," at one of the little tables. Agnes, after many vain attempts to draw Rachel's unmanageable brother into conversation, gave it up at last, and sat still by Rachel's side in embarrassed silence. Mamma betook herself steadily to her work-basket. The conversation fell away into mere questions addressed to Louis, and answers in monosyllables, so that it was an extreme relief to every member of the little party when this impracticable visitor rose at last, bowed to them all, and hastened away.

Rachel sat perfectly silent till the sound of his steps had died upon the road; then she burst out in a vehement apologetic outcry. "Oh, don't be angry with him—don't, please," said Rachel; "he thinks I have been trying to persuade you to be kind to him, and he cannot bear *that* even from me; and indeed, indeed you may believe me, it is quite true! I never saw him, except once or twice, in such a humour before."

"My dear," said Mrs Atheling, with that dignified tone which Mamma could assume when it was necessary, to the utter discomfiture of her opponent—"my dear, we are very glad to see your brother, but of course it can be nothing whatever to us the kind of humour he is in; that is quite his own concern."

Poor Rachel now, having no other resource, cried. She was only herself in this uncomfortable moment. She could no longer remember Louis's pride or Louis's dignity; for a moment the poor little subject heart felt a pang of resentment against the object of its idolatry, such as little Rachel had sometimes felt when Louis was "naughty," and she, his unfortunate little shadow, innocently shared in his punishment; but now, as at every former time, the personal trouble of the patient little sister yielded to the dread that Louis "was not understood." "You will know him better some time," she said, drying her sorrowful appealing eyes. So far as appearances went at this moment, it did not seem quite desirable to know him better, and nobody said a word in return.

After this the three girls went out together to the garden, still lying sweet in the calm of the long summer twilight, under a young moon and some early stars. They did not speak a great deal. They were all considerably absorbed with thoughts of this same hero, who, after all, had not taken an effective method of keeping their interest alive.

And Marian did not know how or whence it was that this doubtful and uncertain paladin came to her side in the pleasant darkness, but was startled by his voice in her ear as she leaned once more over the low garden-gate. "It was here I saw you first," said Louis, and Marian's heart leaped in her breast, half with the suddenness of the words, half with—something else. Louis, who had been so haughty and ungracious all the evening—Louis, Rachel's idol, everybody's superior—yet he spoke low in the startled ear of Marian, as if that first seeing had been an era in his life.

"Come with us," said Louis, as Rachel at sight of him hastened to get her bonnet—"come along this enchanted road a dozen steps into fairyland, and back again. I forget everything, even myself, on such a night."

And they went, scarcely answering, yet more satisfied with this brief reference to their knowledge of him, than if the king had forsaken his nature, and become as confidential as Rachel. They went their dozen steps on what was merely the terraced pathway, soft, dark, and grassy, to Agnes and Rachel, who went first in anxious conversation, but which the other two, coming silently behind, had probably a different idea of. Marian at least could not help cogitating these same adjectives, with a faint inquiry within herself, what it was which could make this an enchanted road or fairyland.

CHAPTER XXII
A BEGINNING

The next morning, while the mother and daughters were still in the full fervour of discussion about this same remarkable Louis, he himself was seen for the first time in the early daylight passing the window, with that singular rapidity of step which he possessed in common with his sister. They ceased their argument after seeing him—why, no one could have told; but quite unresolved as the question was, and though Mamma's first judgment, unsoftened by that twilight walk, was still decidedly unfavourable to Louis, they all dropped the subject tacitly and at once. Then Mamma went about various domestic occupations; then Agnes dropped into the chair which stood before that writing-book upon the table, and, with an attention much broken and distracted, gradually fell away into her own ideal world; and then Marian, leading Bell and Beau with meditative hands, glided forth softly to the garden, with downcast face and drooping eyes, full of thought. The children ran away from her at once when their little feet touched the grass, but Marian went straying along the paths, absorbed in her meditation, her pretty arms hanging by her side, her pretty head bent, her light fair figure gliding softly in shadow over the low mossy paling and the close-clipped hedge within. She was thinking only what it was most natural she should think, about the stranger of last night; yet now and then into the stream of her musing dropped, with the strangest disturbance and commotion, these few quiet words spoken in her ear,—"It was here I saw you first." How many times, then, had Louis seen her? and why did he recollect so well that first occasion? and what did he mean?

While she was busy with these fancies, all at once, Marian could not tell how, as suddenly as he appeared last night, Louis was here again—here, within the garden of the Old Wood Lodge, walking by Marian's side, a second long shadow upon the close-clipped hedge and the mossy paling, rousing her to a guilty consciousness that she had been thinking of him, which brought blush after blush in a flutter of "sweet shamefacednesse" to her cheek, and weighed down still more heavily the shy and dreamy lids of these beautiful eyes.

The most unaccountable thing in the world! but Marian, who had received with perfect coolness the homage of Sir Langham, and whose conscience smote her with no compunctions for the slaying of the gifted American, had strangely lost her self-possession to-day. She only replied in the sedatest and gravest manner possible to the questions of her companion—looked anxiously at the parlour window for an opportunity of calling Agnes, and with the greatest embarrassment longed for the presence of some one to end this *tête-à-tête*. Louis, on the contrary, exerted himself for her amusement, and was as different from the Louis of last night as it was possible to conceive.

"Ay, there it is," said Louis, who had just asked her what she knew of Oxford—"there it is, the seat of learning, thrusting up all its pinnacles to the sun; but I think, if the world were wise, this glitter and shining might point to the dark, dark ignorance outside of it, even more than to the little glow within."

Now this was not much in Marian's way—but her young squire, who would have submitted himself willingly to her guidance had she given any, was not yet acquainted at all with the ways of Marian.

She said, simply looking at the big dome sullenly throwing off the sunbeams, and at the glancing arrowheads, of more impressible and delicate kind, "I think it is very pretty, with all those different spires and towers; but do you mean it is the poor people who are so very ignorant? It seems as though people could scarcely help learning who live there."

"Yes, the poor people—I mean all of us," said Louis slowly, and with a certain painful emphasis. "A great many of the villagers, it is true, have never been to school; but I do not count a man ignorant who knows what he has to do, and how to do it, though he never reads a book, nor has pen in hand all his life. I save my pity for a more unfortunate ignorance than that."

"But that is very bad," said Marian decidedly, "because there is more to do than just to work, and we ought to know about—about a great many things. Agnes knows better than I."

This was said very abruptly, and meant that Agnes knew better what Marian meant to say than she herself did. The youth at her side, however, showed no inclination for any interpreter. He seemed, indeed, to be rather pleased than otherwise with this breaking off.

"When I was away, I was in strange enough quarters, and learnt something about knowledge," said Louis, "though not much knowledge itself—heaven help me! I suppose I was not worthy of that."

"And did you really run away?" asked Marian, growing bolder with this quickening of personal interest.

"I really ran away," said the young man, a hot flush passing for an instant over his brow; and then he smiled—a kind of daring desperate smile, which seemed to say "what I have done once I can do again."

"And what did you do?" said Marian, continuing her inquiries: she forgot her shyness in following up this story, which she knew and did not know.

"What all the village lads do who get into scrapes and break the hearts of the old women," said Louis, with a somewhat bitter jesting. "I listed for a soldier—but there was not even an old woman to break her heart for me."

"Oh, there was Rachel!" cried Marian eagerly.

"Yes, indeed, there was Rachel, my good little sister," answered the young man; "but her kind heart would have mended again had they let me alone. It would have been better for us both."

He said this with a painful compression of his lip, which a certain wistful sympathy in the mind of Marian taught her to recognise as the sign of tumult and contention in this turbulent spirit. She hastened with a womanly instinct to direct him to the external circumstances again.

"And you were really a soldier—a—not an officer—only a common man." Marian shrunk visibly from this, which was an actual and possible degradation, feared as the last downfall for the "wild sons" of the respectable families in the neighbourhood of Bellevue.

"Yes, I belong to a class which has no privileges; there was not a drummer in the regiment but was of better birth than I," exclaimed Louis. "Ah, that is folly—I did very well. In Napoleon's army, had I belonged to that day!—but in my time there was neither a general nor a war."

"Surely," said Marian, who began to be anxious about this unfortunate young man's "principles," "you would not wish for a war?"

"Should you think it very wrong?" said Louis with a smile.

"Yes," answered the young Mentor with immediate decision; for this conversation befell in those times, not so very long ago, when everybody declared that such convulsions were over, and that it was impossible, in the face of civilisation, steamboats, and the electric telegraph, to entertain the faintest idea of a war.

They had reached this point in their talk, gradually growing more at ease and familiar with each other, when it suddenly chanced that Mamma, passing from her own sleeping-room to that of the girls, paused a moment to look out at the small middle window in the passage between them, and looking down, was amazed to see this haughty and misanthropic Louis passing quietly along the trim pathway of the garden, keeping his place steadily by Marian's side. Mrs Atheling was not a mercenary mother, neither was she one much given to alarm for her daughters, lest they should make bad marriages or fall into unfortunate love; but Mrs Atheling, who was scrupulously proper, did not like to see her pretty Marian in such friendly companionship with "a young man in such an equivocal position," even though he was the brother of her friend. "We may be kind to them," said Mamma to herself, "but we are not to go any further; and, indeed, it would be very sad if he should come to more grief about Marian, poor young man;—how pretty she is!"

Yes, it was full time Mrs Atheling should hasten down stairs, and, in the most accidental manner in the world, step out into the garden. Marian, unfortunate child! with her young roses startled on her sweet young cheeks by this faint presaging breath of a new existence, had never been so pretty all her life.

CHAPTER XXIII
THE YOUNG PEOPLE

What Louis did or said, or how he made interest for himself in the tender heart of Mamma, no one very well knows; yet a certain fact it was, that from henceforward Mrs Atheling, like Miss Anastasia, became somewhat contemptuous of Rachel in the interest of Louis, and pursued eager and long investigations in her own mind—investigations most fruitless, yet most persevering—touching the old lord and the unknown conclusion of his life. All that was commonly known of the last years of the last Lord Winterbourne was, that he had died abroad. Under the pressure of family calamity he had gone to Italy, and there, people said, had wandered about for several years, leading a desultory and unsettled life, entirely out of the knowledge of any of his friends; and when the present bearer of the title came home, bearing the intelligence of his elder brother's death, the most entire oblivion closed down upon the foreign grave of the old lord. Back into this darkness Mrs Atheling, who knew no more than common report, made vain efforts to strain her kindly eyes, but always returned with a sigh of despair. "No!" said Mamma, "he might be proud, but he was virtuous and honourable. I never heard a word said against the old lord. Louis is like him, but it must only be a chance resemblance. No! Mr Reginald was always a wild bad man. Poor things! they *must* be his children; for my lord, I am sure, never betrayed or deceived any creature all his life."

But still she mused and dreamed concerning Louis; he seemed to exercise a positive fascination over all these elder people; and Mrs Atheling, more than she had ever desired a friendly gossip with Miss Willsie, longed to meet once more with the Honourable Anastasia, to talk over her conjectures and guesses respecting "the boy."

In the mean time, Louis himself, relieved from that chaperonship and anxious introduction by his sister, which the haughty young man could not endure, made daily increase of his acquaintance with the strangers. He began to form part of their daily circle, expected and calculated upon; and somehow the family life seemed to flow in a stronger and fuller current with the addition of this vigorous element, the young man, who oddly enough seemed to belong to them rather more than if he had been their brother.

He took the three girls, who were now so much like three sisters, on long and wearying excursions through the wood and over the hill. He did not mind tiring them out, nor was he extremely fastidious about the roads by which he led them; for, generous at heart as he was, the young man had the unconscious wilfulness of one who all his life had known no better guidance than his own will. Sometimes, in those long walks of theirs, the young Athelings were startled by some singular characteristic of their squire, bringing to light in him, by a sudden chance, things of which these gentle-hearted girls had never dreamed. Once they discovered, lying deep among the great fern-leaves, all brown and rusty with seed, the bright plumage of some dead game, for the reception of which a village boy was making a bag of his pinafore. "Carry it openly," said Louis, at whose voice the lad started; "and if any one asks you where it came from, send them to me." This was his custom, which all the village knew and profited by; he would not permit himself to be restrained from the sport, but he scorned to lift the slain bird, which might be supposed to be Lord Winterbourne's, and left it to be picked up by the chance foragers of the hamlet. At the first perception of this, the girls, we are obliged to confess, were greatly shocked—tears even came to Marian's eyes. She said it was cruel, in a little outbreak of terror, pity, and indignation. "Cruel—no!" said Louis: "did my gun give a sharper wound than one of the score of fashionable guns that will be waking all the echoes in a day or two?" But Marian only glanced up at him hurriedly with her shy eyes, and said, with a half smile, "Perhaps though the wound was no sharper, the poor bird might have liked another week of life."

And the young man looked up into the warm blue sky over-head, all crossed and trellised with green leaves, and looked around into the deep September foliage, flaming here and there in a yellow leaf, a point of fire among the green. "I think it very doubtful," he said, sinking his voice, though every one heard him among the noonday hush of the trees, "if I ever can be so happy again. Do you not suppose it would be something worth living for, instead of a week or a year of sadder chances, to be shot upon the wing *now*?"

Marian did not say a word, but shrank away among the bushes, clinging to Rachel's arm, with a shy instinctive motion. "Choose for yourself," said Agnes; "but do not decide so coolly upon the likings of the poor bird. I am sure, had *he* been consulted, he would rather have taken his chance of the guns next week than lain so quiet under the fern-leaves now."

Whereupon the blush of youth for his own super-elevated and unreal sentiment came over Louis's face. Agnes, by some amusing process common to young girls who are elder sisters, and whom nobody is in love with, had made herself out to be older than Louis, and was rather disposed now and then to interfere for the regulation of this youth's improper sentiments, and to give him good advice.

And Lord Winterbourne arrived: they discovered the fact immediately by the entire commotion and disturbance of everything about the village, by the noise of wheels, and the flight of servants, to be descried instantly in the startled neighbourhood. Then they began to see visions of sportsmen, and flutters of fine ladies; and even without these visible and evident signs, it would have been easy enough to read the information of the arrivals in the clouded and lowering brow of Louis, and in poor little Rachel's distress, anxiety, and agitation. She, poor child, could no longer join their little kindly party in the evening; and when her brother came without her, he burst into violent outbreaks of rage, indignation, and despair, dreadful to see. Neither mother nor daughters knew how to soothe him; for it was even more terrible in their fancy than in his experience to be the Pariah and child of degradation in this great house. Moved by the intolerable burden of this his time of trial, Louis at last threw himself upon the confidence of his new friends, confided his uncertain and conflicting plans to them, relieved himself of his passionate resentment, and accepted their sympathy. Every day he came goaded half to madness, vowing his determination to bear it no longer; but every day, as he sat in the old easy-chair, with his handsome head half-buried in his hands, a solace, sweet and indescribable, stole into Louis's heart; he was inspired to go at the very same moment that he was impelled to stay, by that same vision which he had first seen in the summer twilight at the old garden-gate.

CHAPTER XXIV
A MEETING

This state of things continued for nearly a fortnight after the arrival of Lord Winterbourne and his party at the Hall. They saw Mrs Edgerley passing through the village, and in church; but she either did not see them, or did not think it necessary to take any notice of the girls. Knowing better now the early connection between their own family and Lord Winterbourne's, they were almost glad of this—almost; yet certainly it would have been pleasanter to decline *her* friendly advances, than to find her, their former patroness, quietly dropping acquaintance with *them*.

The grassy terraced road which led from Winterbourne village to the highway, and which was fenced on one side by the low wall which surrounded the stables and outhouses of the Rector, and by the hedge and paling of the Old Wood Lodge, but on the other side was free and open to the fields, which sloped down from it to the low willow-dropped banks of one of those pale rivers, was not a road adapted either for vehicles or horses. The Rivers family, however, holding themselves monarchs of all they surveyed, stood upon no punctilio in respect to the pathway of the villagers, and the family temper, alike in this one particular, brought about a collision important enough to all parties concerned, and especially to the Athelings; for one of those days, when a riding-party from the Hall cantered along the path with a breezy waving and commotion of veils and feathers and riding-habits, and a pleasant murmur of sound, voices a little louder than usual under cover of the September gale mixed only with the jingle of the harness— for the horses' hoofs struck no sound but that of a dull tread from the turf of the way—it pleased Miss Anastasia, at the very hour and moment of their approach, to drive her two grey ponies to the door of the Old Wood Lodge. Of course, it was the simplest "accident" in the world, this unpremeditated "chance" meeting. There was no intention nor foresight whatever in the matter. When she saw them coming, Miss Anastasia "growled" under her breath, and marvelled indignantly how they could dream of coming in such a body over the grassed road of the villagers, cutting it to pieces with their horses' hoofs. She never paused to consider how the wheels of her own substantial vehicle ploughed the road; and for her part, the leader of the fair equestrians brightened with an instant hope of amusement. "Here is cousin Anastasia, the most learned old lady in Banburyshire. Delightful! Now, my love, you shall see the lion of the county," cried Mrs Edgerley to one of her young companions, not thinking nor caring whether her voice reached her kinswoman or not. Lord Winterbourne, who was with his daughter, drew back to the rear of the group instinctively. Whatever was said of Lord Winterbourne, his worst enemy could not say that he was brave to meet the comments of those whom he had harmed or wronged.

Miss Anastasia stepped from her carriage in the most deliberate manner possible, nodded to Marian and Agnes, who were in the garden—and to whose defence, seeing so many strangers, hastily appeared their mother— and stood patting and talking to her ponies, in her brown cloth pelisse and tippet, and with that oddest of comfortable bonnets upon her head.

"Cousin Anastasia, I vow! You dear creature, where have you been all these ages? Would any one believe it? Ah, how delightful to live always in the country; what a penalty we pay for town and its pleasures! Could any one suppose that my charming cousin was actually older than me?"

And the fashionable beauty, though she did begin to be faded, threw up her delicate hands with their prettiest gesture, as she pointed to the stately old lady before her, in her antique dress, and with unconcealed furrows in her face. Once, perhaps, not even that beautiful complexion of Mrs Edgerley was sweeter than that of Anastasia Rivers; but her beauty had gone from her long ago—a thing which she cared not to retain. She looked up with her kind imperious face, upon which were undeniable marks of years and age. She perceived with a most evident and undisguised contempt the titter with which this comparison was greeted. "Go on your way, Louisa," said Miss Rivers; "you were pretty once, whatever people say of you now. Don't be a fool, child; and I advise you not to meddle with me."

"Delightful! is she not charming?" cried the fine lady, appealing to her companion; "so fresh, and natural, and eccentric—such an acquisition in the Hall! Anastasia, dear, do forget your old quarrel. It was not poor papa's fault that you were born a woman, though I cannot help confessing it was a great mistake, *certainly*; but, only for once, you who are such a dear, kind, benevolent creature, come to see *me*."

"Go on, Louisa, I advise you," said the Honourable Anastasia with extreme self-control. "Poor child, I have no quarrel with you, at all events. You did not choose your father—there, pass on. I leave the Hall to those who choose it; the Old Wood Lodge has more attraction for me."

"And I protest," cried Mrs Edgerley, "it is my sweet young friend, the author of — —: my dearest child, what *is* the name of your book? I have *such* a memory. Quite the sweetest story of the season; and I am dying to hear of another. Are you writing again? Oh, pray say you are. I should be heartbroken to think of waiting very long for it. You must come to the Hall. There are some people coming who are dying to know you, and I positively cannot be disappointed: no one ever disobeys *me*! Come here and let me kiss, you pretty creature. Is she not the sweetest little beauty in the world? and her sister has so much genius; it is quite delightful! So you know my cousin Anastasia; isn't she charming? Now, good morning, coz.—good morning, dear—and be sure you come to the Hall."

Miss Anastasia stood aside, watching grimly this unexpected demonstration of friendship, and keenly criticising Agnes, who coloured high with youthful dignity and resentment, and Marian, who drew back abashed, with a painful blush, and a grieved and anxious consciousness that Louis, unseen but seeing, was a spectator of this salutation, and somehow would be quite as like to resent Mrs Edgerley's careless compliment to herself, "as if I had been his sister." With a steady observation the old lady kept her eyes upon her young acquaintances till the horsemen and horsewomen of Mrs Edgerley's train had passed. Then she drew herself up to the utmost pitch of her extreme height, and, without raising her eyes, made a profound curtsy to the last of the train—he on his part lifted his hat, and bent to his saddle-bow. This was how Lord Winterbourne and his brother's daughter recognised each other. Perhaps the wandering eyes in his bloodless face glanced a moment, shifting and uncertain as they were, upon the remarkable figure of Miss Rivers, but they certainly paused to take in, with one fixed yet comprehensive glance, the mother and the daughters, the children playing in the garden—the open door of the house—even it was possible he saw Louis, though Louis had been behind, at the end of the little green, out of sight, trying to train a wild honeysuckle round an extempore bower. Lord Winterbourne scarcely paused, and did not offer the slightest apology for his stare, but they felt, all of them, that he had marked the house, and laid them under the visionary curse of his evil eye. When he had passed, Miss Rivers put them in before her, with an imperative gesture. "Let me know what's brewing," said the Honourable Anastasia, as she reposed herself on the little new sofa in the old parlour. "There's mischief in his eye."

CHAPTER XXV
THE BREWING OF THE STORM

The visit of Miss Rivers was the most complimentary attention which she could show to her new friends, for her visits were few, and paid only to a very limited number of people, and these all of her own rank and class. She was extremely curious as to their acquaintance with Mrs Edgerley, and demanded to know every circumstance from its beginning until now; and this peremptory old lady was roused to quite an eager and animated interest in the poor little book of which, Agnes could not forget, Mrs Edgerley did not remember so much as the name. The Honourable Anastasia declared abruptly that she never read novels, yet demanded to have *Hope Hazlewood* placed without an instant's delay in her pony-carriage. "Do it at once, my dear: a thing which is done at the moment cannot be forgotten," said Miss Rivers. "You write books, eh? Well, I asked you if you were clever; why did you not tell me at once?"

"I did not think you would care; it was not worth while," said Agnes with some confusion, and feeling considerably alarmed by the idea of this formidable old lady's criticism. Miss Rivers only answered by hurrying her out with the book, lest it might possibly be forgotten. When the girls were gone, she turned to Mrs Atheling. "What can he do to you," said Miss Anastasia, abruptly, "eh? What's Will Atheling doing? Can he harm Will?"

"No," said Mamma, somewhat excited by the prospect of an enemy, yet confident in the perfect credit and honour of the family father, whose good name and humble degree of prosperity no enemy could overthrow. "William has been where he is now for twenty years."

"So, so," said Miss Rivers—"and the boy? Take care of these girls; it might be in his devilish way to harm them; and I tell you, when you come to know of it, send me word. So she writes books, this girl of yours? She is no better than a child. Do you mean to say you are not proud?"

Mrs Atheling answered as mothers answer when such questions are put to them, half with a confession, half with a partly-conscious sophism, about Agnes being "a good girl, and a great comfort to her papa and me."

The girls, when they had executed their commission, looked doubtingly for Louis, but found him gone as they expected. While they were still lingering where he had been, Miss Rivers came to the door again, going away, and when she had said good-by to Mamma, the old lady turned back again without a word, and very gravely gathered one of the roses. She did it with a singular formality and solemness as if it was a religious observance rather than a matter of private liking; and securing it somewhere out of sight in the fastenings of her brown pelisse, waved her hand to them, saying in her peremptory voice, quite loud enough to be heard at a considerable distance, that she was to send for them in a day or two. Then she took her seat in the little carriage, and turned her grey ponies, no very easy matter, towards the high-road. Her easy and complete mastery over them was an admiration to the girls. "Bless you, miss, she'd follow the hounds as bold as any squire," said Hannah; "but there's a deal o' difference in Miss Taesie since the time she broke her heart."

Such an era was like to be rather memorable. The girls thought so, somewhat solemnly, as they went to their work beside their mother. They seemed to be coming to graver times themselves, gliding on in an irresistible noiseless fashion upon their stream of fate.

Louis came again as usual in the evening. He *had* heard Mrs Edgerley, and did resent her careless freedom, as Marian secretly knew he would; which fact she who was most concerned, ascertained by his entire and pointed silence upon the subject, and his vehement and passionate contempt, notwithstanding, for Mrs Edgerley.

"I suppose you are safe enough," he said, speaking to the elder sister. "You will not break your heart because she has forgotten the name of your book—but, heaven help them, there are hearts which do! There are unfortunate fools in this crazy world mad enough to be elated and to be thrown into misery by a butterfly of a fine lady, who makes reputations. You think them quite contemptible, do you? but there are such."

"I suppose they must be people who have no friends and no home—or to whom it is of more importance than it is to me," said Agnes; "for I am only a woman, and nothing could make me miserable out of this Old Lodge, or Bellevue."

"Ah—that is *now*," said Louis quickly, and he glanced with an instinctive reference at Marian, whose pallid roses and fluctuating mood already began to testify to some anxiety out of the boundary of these charmed walls. "The very sight of your security might possibly be hard enough upon us who have no home—no home! nothing at all under heaven."

"Except such trifles as strength and youth and a stout heart, a sister very fond of you, and some—some *friends*—and heaven itself, after all, at the end. Oh, Louis!" said Agnes, who on this, as on other occasions, was much disposed to be this "boy's" elder sister, and advised him "for his good."

He did not say anything. When he looked up at all from his bending attitude leaning over the table, it was to glance with fiery devouring eyes at Marian—poor little sweet Marian, already pale with anxiety for him. Then he broke out suddenly—"That poor little sister who is very fond of me—do you know what she is doing at this moment—singing to them!—like the captives at Babylon, making mirth for the spoilers. And my friends——heaven! you heard what that woman ventured to say to-day."

"My dear," said Mrs Atheling, who confessed to treating Louis as a "son of her own," "think of heaven all the day long, and so much the better for you—but I cannot have you using in this way such a name."

This simple little reproof did more for Louis than a hundred philosophies. He laughed low, and with emotion took Mrs Atheling's hand for a moment between his own—said "thank you, mother," with a momentary smile of delight and good pleasure. Then his face suddenly flushed with a dark and violent colour; he cast an apprehensive yet haughty glance at Mrs Atheling, and drew his hand away. The stain in his blood was a ghost by the side of Louis, and scarcely left him for an instant night nor day.

When he left them, they went to the door with him as they had been wont to do, the mother holding a shawl over her cap, the girls with their fair heads uncovered to the moon. They stood all together at the gate speaking cheerfully, and sending kind messages to Rachel as they bade him good-night—and none of the little group noticed a figure suddenly coming out of the darkness and gliding along past the paling of the garden. "What, boy, you here?" cried a voice suddenly behind Louis, which made him start aside, and they all shrank back a little to recognise in the moonlight the marble-white face of Lord Winterbourne.

"What do you mean, sir, wandering about the country at this hour?" said the stranger—"what conspiracy goes on here, eh?—what are *you* doing with a parcel of women? Home to your den, you skulking young vagabond—what are you doing here?"

Marian, the least courageous of the three, moved by a sudden impulse, which was not courage but terror, laid her hand quickly upon Louis's arm. The young man, who had turned his face defiant and furious towards the intruder, turned in an instant, grasping at the little timid hand as a man in danger might grasp at a shield invulnerable, "You perceive, my lord, I am beyond the reach either of your insults or your patronage here," said the youth, whose blood was dancing in his veins, and who at that moment cared less than the merest stranger, who had never heard his name, for Lord Winterbourne.

"Come, my lad, if you are imposing upon these poor people—I must set you right," said the man who was called Louis's father. "Do you know what he is, my good woman, that you harbour this idle young rascal in despite of my known wishes? Home, you young vagabond, home! This boy is——"

"My lord, my lord," interposed Mrs Atheling, in sudden agitation, "if any disgrace belongs to him, it is yours and not his that you should publish it. Go away, sir, from my door, where you once did harm enough, and don't try to injure the poor boy—perhaps we know who he is better than you."

What put this bold and rash speech into the temperate lips of Mamma, no one could ever tell; the effect of it, however, was electric. Lord Winterbourne fell back suddenly, stared at her with his strained eyes in the moonlight, and swore a muttered and inaudible oath. "Home, you hound!" he repeated in a mechanical tone, and then, waving his hand with a threatening and unintelligible gesture, turned to go away. "So long as the door is yours, my friend, I will take care to make no intrusion upon it," he said significantly before he disappeared; and then the shadow departed out of the moonlight, the stealthy step died on the grass, and they stood alone again with beating hearts. Mamma took Marian's hand from Louis, but not unkindly, and with an affectionate earnestness bade him go away. He hesitated long, but at length consented, partly for her entreaty, partly for the sake of Rachel. Under other circumstances this provocation would have maddened Louis; but he wrung Agnes's hand with an excited gaiety as he lingered at the door watching a shadow on the window whither Marian had gone with her mother. "I had best not meet him on the road," said Louis: "there is the Curate—for once, for your sake, and the sake of what has happened, I will be gracious and take his company; but to tell the truth, I do not care for anything which can befall me to-night."

CHAPTER XXVI
A CRISIS

Marian, whom her mother tenderly put to sleep that night, as if she had been a child, yet who lay awake in the long cold hours before the dawn in a vague and indescribable emotion, her heart stirring within her like something which did not belong to her—a new and strange existence—slept late the next morning, exhausted and worn out with all this sudden and stormy influx of unknown feelings. Mamma, who, on the contrary, was very early astir, came into the bed-chamber of her daughters at quite an unusual hour, and, thankfully perceiving Marian's profound youthful slumber, stood gazing at the beautiful sleeper with tears in her eyes. Paler than usual, with a shadow under her closed eyelids, and still a little dew upon the long lashes—with one hand laid in childish fashion under her cheek, and the other lying, with its pearly rose-tipped fingers, upon the white coverlid, Marian, but for the moved and human agitation which evidently had worn itself into repose, might have looked like the enchanted beauty of the tale—but indeed she was rather more like a child who had wept itself to sleep. Her sister, stealing softly from her side, left her sleeping, and they put the door ajar that they might hear when she stirred before they went, with hushed steps and speaking in a whisper, down stairs.

Mrs Atheling was disturbed more than she would tell; what she did say, as Agnes and she sat over their silent breakfast-table, was an expedient which herself had visibly no faith in. "My dear, we must try to prevent him saying anything," said Mrs Atheling, with her anxious brow: it was not necessary to name names, for neither of them could forget the scene of last night.

Then by-and-by Mamma spoke again. "I almost fancy we should go home; she might forget it if she were away. Agnes, my love, you must persuade him not to say anything; he pays great attention to what you say."

"But, mamma—Marian?" said Agnes.

"Oh, Agnes, Agnes, my dear beautiful child," said Mrs Atheling, with a sudden access of emotion, "it was only friendship, sympathy—her kind heart; she will think no more of it, if nothing occurs to put it into her head."

Agnes did not say anything, though she was extremely doubtful on this subject; but then it was quite evident that Mamma had no faith in her own prognostications, and regarded this first inroad into the family with a mixture of excitement, dread, and agitation which it was not comfortable to see.

After their pretended breakfast, mother and daughter once more stole up-stairs. They had not been in the room a moment, when Marian woke— woke—started with fright and astonishment to see Agnes dressed, and her mother standing beside her; and beginning to recollect, suddenly blushed, and turning away her face, burning with that violent suffusion of colour, exclaimed, "I could not help it—I could not help it; would you stand by and see them drive him mad? Oh mamma, mamma!"

"My darling, no one thinks of blaming you," said Mrs Atheling, who trembled a good deal, and looked very anxious. "We were all very sorry for him, poor fellow; and you only did what you should have done, like a brave little friend—what I should have done myself, had I been next to him," said Mamma, with great gravity and earnestness, but decidedly overdoing her part.

This did not seem quite a satisfactory speech to Marian. She turned away again petulantly, dried her eyes, and with a sidelong glance at Agnes, asked, "Why did you not wake me?—it looks quite late. I am not ill, am I? I am sure I do not understand it—why did you let me sleep?"

"Hush, darling! because you were tired and late last night," said Mamma.

Now this sympathy and tenderness seemed rather alarming than soothing to Marian. Her colour varied rapidly, her breath came quick, tears gathered to her eyes. "Has anything happened while I have been sleeping?" she asked hastily, and in a very low tone.

"No, no, my love, nothing at all," said Mamma tenderly, "only we thought you must be tired."

"Both you and Agnes were as late as me,—why were not you tired?" said Marian, still with a little jealous fear. "Please, mamma, go away; I want to get dressed and come down stairs."

They left her to dress accordingly, but still with some anxiety and apprehension, and Mamma waited for Marian in her own room, while Agnes went down to the parlour—just in time, for as she took her seat, Louis, flushed and impatient, burst in at the door.

Louis made a most hasty salutation, and was a great deal too eager and hurried to be very well bred. He looked round the room with sudden anxiety and disappointment. "Where is she?—I must see Marian," cried Louis. "What! you do not mean to say she is ill, after last night?"

"Not ill, but in her own room," said Agnes, somewhat confused by the question.

"I will wait as long as you please, if I must wait," said Louis impatiently; "but, Agnes! why should you be against me? Of course, I forget myself; do you grudge that I should? I forget everything except last night; let me see Marian. I promise you I will not distress her, and if she bids me, I will go away."

"No, it is not that," said Agnes with hesitation; "but, Louis, nothing happened last night—pray do not think of it. Well, then," she said earnestly, as his hasty gesture denied what she said, "mamma begs you, Louis, not to say anything to-day."

He turned round upon her with a blank but haughty look. "I understand—my disgrace must not come here," he said; "but *she* did not mind it; she, the purest lily upon earth! Ah! so that was a dream, was it? And her mother—her mother says I am to go away?"

"No, indeed—no," said Agnes, almost crying. "No, Louis, you know better; do not misunderstand us. She is so young, so gentle, and tender. Mamma only asked, for all our sakes, if you would consent not to say anything *now*."

To this softened form of entreaty the eager young man paid not the slightest attention. He began to use the most unblushing cajolery to win over poor Agnes. It did not seem to be Louis; so entirely changed was his demeanour. It was only an extremely eager and persevering specimen of the genus "lover," without any personal individuality at all.

"What! not say anything? Could anybody ask such a sacrifice?" cried this wilful and impetuous youth. "It might, as you say, be nothing at all, though it seems life—existence, to me. Not know whether that hand is mine or another's—that hand which saved me, perhaps from murder?—for he is an old man, though he is a fiend incarnate, and I might have killed him where he stood."

"Louis! Louis!" cried Agnes, gazing at him in terror and excitement. He grew suddenly calm as he caught her eye.

"It is quite true," he said with a grave and solemn calmness. "This man, who has cursed my life, and made it miserable—this man, who dared insult me before *her* and you—do you think I could have been a man, and still have borne that intolerable crown of wrong?"

As he spoke, he began to pace the little parlour with impatient steps and a clouded brow. Mrs Atheling, who had heard his voice, but had restrained her anxious curiosity as long as possible, now came down quietly, unable to keep back longer. Louis sprang to her side, took her hand, led her about the room, pleading, reasoning, persuading. Mamma, whose good heart from the first moment had been an entire and perfect traitor, was no match at all for Louis. She gave in to him unresistingly before half his entreaties were over; she did not make even half so good a stand as Agnes, who secretly was in the young lover's interest too. But when they had just come to the conclusion that he should be permitted to see Marian, Marian herself, whom no one expected, suddenly entered the room. The young beauty's pretty brow was lowering more than any one before had ever seen it lower; a petulant contraction was about her red lips, and a certain angry dignity, as of an offended child, in her bearing. "Surely something very strange has happened this morning," said Marian, with a little heat; "even mamma looks as if she knew some wonderful secret. I suppose every one is to hear of it but me."

At this speech the dismayed conspirators against Marian's peace fell back and separated. The other impetuous principal in the matter hastened at once to the angry Titania, who only bowed, and did not even look at him. The truth was, that Marian, much abashed at thought of her own sudden impulse, was never in a mood less propitious; she felt as if she herself had not done quite right—as if somehow she had betrayed a secret of her own, and, now found out and detected, was obliged to use the readiest means to cover it up again; and, besides, the hasty little spirit, which had both pride and temper of its own, could not at all endure the idea of having been petted and excused this morning, as if "something had happened" last night. Now that it was perfectly evident nothing had happened—now that Louis stood before her safe, handsome, and eager, Marian concluded that it was time for her to stand upon her defence.

CHAPTER XXVII
CLOUDS

The end of it all was, of course—though Louis had an amount of trouble in the matter which that impetuous young gentleman had not counted upon—that Marian yielded to his protestations, and came forth full of the sweetest agitation, tears, and blushes, to be taken to the kind breast of the mother who was scarcely less agitated, and to be regarded with a certain momentary awe, amusement, and sympathy by Agnes, whose visionary youthful reverence for this unknown magician was just tempered by the equally youthful imp of mischief which plays tricks upon the same. But Mrs Atheling's brow grew sadder and sadder with anxiety, as she looked at the young man who now claimed to call her mother. What he was to do—how Marian could bear all the chances and changes of the necessarily long probation before them—what influence Lord Winterbourne might have upon the fortunes of his supposed son—what Papa himself would say to this sudden betrothal, and how he could reconcile himself to receive a child, and a disgraced child of his old enemy, into his own honourable house,—these considerations fluttered the heart and disturbed the peace of the anxious mother, who already began to blame herself heavily, yet did not see, after all, what else she could have done. A son of shame, and of Lord Winterbourne!—a young man hitherto dependent, with no training, no profession, no fortune, of no use in the world. And her prettiest Marian!— the sweet face which won homage everywhere, and which every other face involuntarily smiled to see. Darker and darker grew the cloud upon the brow of Mrs Atheling; she went in, out of sight of these two happy young dreamers, with a sick heart. For the first time in her life she was dismayed at the thought of writing to her husband, and sat idly in a chair drawn back from her window, wearying herself out with most vain and unprofitable speculations as to things which might have been done to avert this fate.

No very long time elapsed, however, before Mrs Atheling found something else to occupy her thoughts. Hannah came in to the parlour, solemnly announcing a man at the door who desired to see her. With a natural presentiment, very naturally arising from the excited state of her own mind, Mrs Atheling rose, and hastened to the door. The man was an attorney's clerk, threadbare and respectable, who gave into her hand an open paper, and after it a letter. The paper, which she glanced over with hasty alarm, was a formal notice to quit, on pain of ejection, from the house called the Old Wood Lodge, the property of Reginald, Lord Winterbourne. "The property of Lord Winterbourne!—it is our—it is my husband's property. What does this mean?" cried Mrs Atheling.

"I know nothing of the business, but Mr Lewis's letter will explain it," said the messenger, who was civil but not respectful; and the anxious mistress of the house hastened in with great apprehension and perplexity to open the letter and see what this explanation was. It was not a very satisfactory one. With a friendly spirit, yet with a most cautious and lawyer-like regard to the interest of his immediate client, Mr Lewis, the same person who had been intrusted with the will of old Miss Bridget, and who was Lord Winterbourne's solicitor, announced the intention of his principal to "resume possession" of Miss Bridget's little house. "You will remember," wrote the lawyer, "that I did not fail to point out to you at the time the insecure nature of the tenure by which this little property was held. Granted, as I believe it was, as a gift simply for the lifetime of Miss Bridget Atheling, she had, in fact, no right to bequeath it to any one, and so much of her will as relates to this is null and void. I am informed that there are documents in existence proving this fact beyond the possibility of dispute, and that any resistance would be entirely vain. As a friend, I should advise you not to attempt it; the property is actually of very small value, and though I speak against the interest of my profession, I think it right to warn you against entering upon an expensive lawsuit with a man like Lord Winterbourne, to whom money is no consideration. For the sake of your family, I appeal to you whether it would not be better, though at a sacrifice of feeling, to give up without resistance the old house, which is of very little value to any one, if it were not for my lord's whim of having no small proprietors in his neighbourhood. I should be sorry that he was made acquainted with this communication. I write to you merely from private feelings, as an old friend."

Mrs Atheling rose from her seat hastily, holding the papers in her hand. "Resist him!" she exclaimed—"yes, certainly, to the very last;" but at that moment there came in at the half-open door a sound of childish riot, exuberant and unrestrained, which arrested the mother's words, and subdued her like a spell. Bell and Beau, rather neglected and thrown into the shade for the first time in their lives, were indemnifying themselves in the kitchen, where they reigned over Hannah with the most absolute and unhesitating mastery. Mamma fell back again into her seat, silent, pale, and with pain and terror in her face. Was this the first beginning of the blight of the Evil Eye?

And then she remained thinking over it sadly and in silence; sometimes, disposed to blame herself for her rashness—sometimes with a natural rising of indignation, disposed to repeat again her first outcry, and resist this piece of oppression—sometimes starting with the sudden fright of an anxious and timid mother, and almost persuaded at once, without further parley, to flee to her own safe home, and give up, without a word, the new inheritance. But she was not learned in the ways of the world, in law, or necessary ceremonial. Resist was a mere vague word to her, meaning she knew not what, and no step occurred to her in the matter but the general necessity for "consulting a lawyer," which was of itself an uncomfortable peril. As she argued with herself, indeed, Mrs Atheling grew quite hopeless, and gave up the whole matter. She had known, through many changes, the success of this bad man, and in her simple mind had no confidence in the abstract power of the law to maintain the cause, however just, of William Atheling, who would have hard ado to pay a lawyer's fees, against Lord Winterbourne.

Then she called in her daughters, whom Louis then only, and with much reluctance, consented to leave, and held a long and agitated counsel with them. The girls were completely dismayed by the news, and mightily impressed by that new and extraordinary "experience" of a real enemy, which captivated Agnes's wandering imagination almost as much as it oppressed her heart. As for Marian, she sat looking at them blankly, turning from Mamma to Agnes, and from Agnes to Mamma, with a vague perception that this was somehow because of Louis, and a very heavy heartbreaking depression in her agitated thoughts. Marian, though she was not very imaginative, had caught a tinge of the universal romance at this crisis of her young life, and, cast down with the instant omen of misfortune, saw clouds and storms immediately rising through that golden future, of which Louis's prophecies had been so pleasant to hear.

And there could be no doubt that this suddenly formed engagement, hasty, imprudent, and ill-advised as it was, added a painful complication to the whole business. If it was known—and who could conceal from the gossip of the village the constant visits of Louis, or his undisguised devotion?— then it would set forth evidently in public opposition the supposed father and son. "But Lord Winterbourne is not his father!" cried Marian suddenly, with tears and vehemence. Mrs Atheling shook her head, and said that people supposed so at least, and this would be a visible sign of war.

But no one in the family counsel could advise anything in this troubled moment. Charlie was coming—that was a great relief and comfort. "If Charlie knows anything, it should be the law," said Mrs Atheling, with a sudden joy in the thought that Charlie had been full six months at it, and ought to be very well informed indeed upon the subject. And then Agnes brought her blotting-book, and the good mother sat down to write the most uncomfortable letter she had ever written to her husband in all these two-and-twenty years. There was Marian's betrothal, first of all, which was so very unlike to please him—he who did not even know Louis, and could form no idea of his personal gifts and compensations—and then there was the news of this summons, and of the active and powerful enemy suddenly started up against them. Mrs Atheling took a very long time composing the letter, but sighed heavily to think how soon Papa would read it, to the destruction of all his pleasant fancies about his little home in the country, and his happy children. Charlie was coming—they had all a certain faith in Charlie, boy though he was; it was the only comfort in the whole prospect to the anxious eyes of Mamma.

CHAPTER XXVIII
THE REV. LIONEL RIVERS

The next day, somewhat to the consternation of this disturbed and troubled family, they were honoured by a most unlooked-for and solemn visit from the Rector. The Rector, in stature, form, and features, considerably resembled Miss Anastasia, and was, as she herself confessed, an undeniable Rivers, bearing all the family features and not a little of the family temper. He seemed rather puzzled himself to give a satisfactory reason for his call—saying solemnly that he thought it right for the priest of the parish to be acquainted with all his parishioners—words which did not come with half so much unction or natural propriety from his curved and disdainful lip, as they would have done from the bland voice of Mr Mead. Then he asked some ordinary questions how they liked the neighbourhood, addressing himself to Mamma, though his very grave and somewhat haughty looks were principally directed to Agnes. Mrs Atheling, in spite of her dislike of the supreme altitude of his churchmanship, had a natural respect for the clergyman, who seemed the natural referee and adviser of people in trouble; and though he was a Rivers, and the next heir after Lord Winterbourne's only son, it by no means followed on that account that the Rector entertained any affectionate leaning towards Lord Winterbourne.

"I knew your old relative very well," said the Rector; "she was a woman of resolute will and decided opinions, though her firmness, I am afraid, was in the cause of error rather than of truth. I believe she always entertained a certain regard for me, connected as she was with the family, though I felt it my duty to warn her against her pernicious principles before her death."

"Her pernicious principles! Was poor Aunt Bridget an unbeliever?" cried Agnes, with an involuntary interest, and yet an equally involuntary and natural spirit of opposition to this stately young man.

"The word is a wide one. No—not an unbeliever, nor even a disbeliever, so far as I am aware," said the churchman, "but, even more dangerous than a positive error of doctrine, holding these fatal delusions concerning private opinion, which have been the bane of the Church."

There was a little pause after this, the unaccustomed audience being somewhat startled, yet quite unprepared for controversy, and standing beside in a little natural awe of the Rector, who ought to know so much better than they did. Agnes alone felt a stirring of unusual pugnacity—for once in her life she almost forgot her natural diffidence, and would have liked nothing better than to throw down her woman's glove to the rampant churchman, and make a rash and vehement onslaught upon him, after the use and wont of feminine controversy.

"My own conviction is," said the Rector with a little solemnity, yet with a dissatisfied and fiery gleam in his eager dark eyes, "that there is no medium between the infallible authority of the Church and the wildest turmoil of heresy. This one rock a man may plant his foot upon—all beyond is a boundless and infinite chaos. Therefore I count it less perilous to be ill-informed or indifferent concerning some portions of the creed, than to be shaken in the vital point of the Church's authority—the only flood-gate that can be closed against the boiling tide of error, which, but for this safeguard, would overpower us all."

Having made this statement, which somehow he enunciated as if it were a solemn duty, Mr Rivers left the subject abruptly, and returned to common things.

"You are acquainted, I understand," he said, with haste and a little emotion, "with my unfortunate young relatives at the Hall?"

The question was so abrupt and unlooked for, that all the three, even Mamma, who was not very much given to blushing, coloured violently. "Louis and Rachel? Yes; we know them very well," said Mrs Atheling, with as much composure as she could summon to meet the emergency—which certainly was not enough to prevent the young clergyman from discovering a rather unusual degree of interest in the good mother's answer. He looked surprised, and turned a hurried glance upon the girls, who were equally confused under his scrutiny. It was impossible to say which was the culprit, if culprit there was. Mr Rivers, who was tall enough at first, visibly grew a little taller, and became still more stately in his demeanour than before.

"I am not given to gossip," he said, with a faint smile, "yet I had heard that they were much here, and had given their confidence to your family. I have not been so favoured myself," he added, with a slight curl of disdain upon his handsome lip. "The youth I know nothing of, except that he has invariably repelled any friendship I could have shown him; but I feel a great interest in the young lady. Had my sister been in better health, we might have offered her an asylum, but that is impossible in our present circumstances. You are doubtless better acquainted with their prospects and intentions than I am. In case of the event which people begin to talk about, what does Lord Winterbourne intend they should do?"

"We have not heard of any event—what is it?" cried Mrs Atheling, very anxiously.

"I have no better information than common report," said the Rector; "yet it is likely enough—and I see no reason to doubt; it is said that Lord Winterbourne is likely to marry again."

They all breathed more freely after this; and poor little Marian, who had been gazing at Mr Rivers with a blanched face and wide-open eyes, in terror of some calamity, drooped forward upon the table by which she was sitting, and hid her face in her hands with sudden relief. Was that all?

"I was afraid you were about to tell us of some misfortune," said Mrs Atheling.

"It is no misfortune, of course; nor do I suppose they are like to be very jealous of a new claimant upon Lord Winterbourne's affections," said the Rector; "but it seems unlikely, under their peculiar and most unhappy circumstances, that they can remain at the Hall."

"Oh, mamma!" exclaimed Marian, in a half whisper, "he will be so very, *very* glad to go away!"

"What I mean," resumed Mr Rivers, who by no means lost this, though he took no immediate notice of it—"what I wish is, that you would kindly undertake to let them know my very sincere wish to be of service to them. I cannot at all approve of the demeanour of the young man—yet there may be excuses for him. If I can assist them in any legitimate way, I beg you to assure them my best endeavours are at their service."

"Thank you, sir, thank you—thank you!" cried Mrs Atheling, faltering, and much moved. "God knows they have need of friends!"

"I suppose so," said the Rector; "it does not often happen—friends are woeful delusions in most cases—and indeed I have little hope of any man who does not stand alone."

"Yet you offer service," said Agnes, unable quite to control her inclination to dispute his dogmatisms; "is not your opinion a contradiction to your kindness?"

"I hold no opinions," said the Rector haughtily, with, for the instant, a superb absurdity almost equal to Mr Endicott: he perceived it himself, however, immediately, reddened, flashed his fiery eyes with a half defiance upon his young questioner, and made an incomprehensible explanation.

"I am as little fortified against self-contradiction as my fellows," said Mr Rivers, "but I eschew vague opinions; they are dangerous for all men, and doubly dangerous in a clergyman. I may be wrong in matters of feeling; opinions I have nothing to do with—they are not in my way."

Again there followed a pause, for no one present was at all acquainted with sentiments like these.

"I am not sure whether we will continue long here," said Mrs Atheling, with a slight hesitation, half afraid of him, yet feeling, in spite of herself, that she could consult no one so suitably as the Rector. "Lord Winterbourne is trying to put us away; he says the house was only given to old Miss Bridget for her life!"

"Ah! but that is false, is it not?" said the Rector without any ceremony.

Mrs Atheling brightened at once. "We think so," she said, encouraged by the perfectly cool tone of this remark, which proved a false statement on the part of my lord no wonder at all to his reverend relative; "but, indeed, the lawyer advises us not to contest the matter, since Lord Winterbourne does not care for expense, and we are not rich. I do not know what my husband will say; but I am sure I will have a great grudge at the law if we are forced, against justice, to leave the Old Wood Lodge."

"Papa says it was once the property of the family, long, long before Aunt Bridget got it from Lord Winterbourne," said Agnes, with a little eagerness. This shadow of ancestry was rather agreeable to the imagination of Agnes.

"And have you done anything—are you doing anything?" said the Hector. "I should be glad to send my own man of business to you; certainly you ought not to give up your property without at least a legal opinion upon the matter."

"We expect my son to-morrow," said Mrs Atheling, with a little pride. "My son, though he is very young, has a great deal of judgment; and then he has been—brought up to the law."

The Rector bowed gravely as he rose. "In that case, I can only offer my good wishes," said the churchman, "and trust that we may long continue neighbours in spite of Lord Winterbourne. My sister would have been delighted to call upon you, had she been able, but she is quite a confirmed invalid. I am very glad to have made your acquaintance. Good morning, madam; good morning, Miss Atheling. I am extremely glad to have met with you."

The smallest shade of emphasis in the world invested with a different character than usual these clergymanly and parochial words: for the double expression of satisfaction was addressed to Agnes; it was to her pointedly that his stately but reverential bow bore reference. He had come to see the family; but he was glad to know Agnes, the intelligent listener who followed his sermons—the eager bright young eyes which flashed warfare and defiance on his solemn deliverances—and, unawares to herself, saw through the pretences of his disturbed and troubled spirit. Lionel Rivers was not very sensitively alive to the beautiful: he saw little to attract his eye, much less his heart, in that pretty drooping Marian, who was to every other observer the sweetest little downcast princess who ever gained the magic succours of a fairy tale. The Rector scarcely turned a passing glance upon her, as she sat in her tender beauty by the table, leaning her beautiful head upon her hands. But with a different kind of observation from that of Mr Agar, he read the bright and constant comment on what he said himself, and what others said, that ran and sparkled in the face of Agnes. She who never had any lovers, had attracted one at least to watch her looks and her movements with a jealous eye. He was not "in love,"—not the smallest hairbreadth in the world. In his present mood, he would gladly have seen her form an order of sisters, benevolent votaresses of St Frideswide, or of some unknown goddess of the medieval world, build an antique house in the "pointed" style, and live a female bishop ruling over the inferior parish, and being ruled over by the clergy. Such a colleague the Rector fancied would be highly "useful," and he had never seen any one whom he could elect to the office with so much satisfaction as Agnes Atheling. How far she would have felt herself complimented by this idea was entirely a different question, and one of which the Rector never thought.

CHAPTER XXIX
CHARLIE

The next day was the day of Charlie's arrival. His mother and sisters looked for him with anxiety, pleasure, and a little nervousness—much concerned about Papa's opinion, and not at all indifferent to Charlie's own. Rachel, who for two days past had been in a state of perfectly flighty and overpowering happiness, joined the Athelings this evening, at the risk of being "wanted" by Mrs Edgerley, and falling under her displeasure, with a perfectly innocent and unconscious disregard of any possible wish on the part of her friends to be alone with their new-come brother. Rachel could form no idea whatever of that half-wished-for, half-dreaded judgment of Papa, the anticipation of which so greatly subdued Marian, and made Mrs Atheling herself so grave and pale. Louis, with a clearer perception of the family crisis, kept away, though, as his sister wisely judged, at no great distance, chewing the cud of desperate and bitter fancy, almost half-repenting, for the moment, of the rash attachment which had put himself and all his disadvantages upon the judicial examination of a father and a brother. The idea of this family committee sitting upon him, investigating and commenting upon his miserable story, galled to the utmost the young man's fiery spirit. He had no real idea whatever of that good and affectionate father, who was to Marian the first of men,—and had not the faintest conception of the big boy. So it was only an abstract father and brother—the most disagreeable of the species—at whom Louis chafed in his irritable imagination. He too had come already out of the first hurried flush of delight and triumph, to consider the step he had taken. Strangely into the joy and pride of the young lover's dream came bitter and heavy spectres of self-reproach and foreboding—he, who had ventured to bind to himself the heart of a sensitive and tender girl—he, who had already thrown a shadow over her young life, filled her with premature anxieties, and communicated to these young eyes, instead of their fearless natural brightness, a wistful forecasting gaze into an adverse world—he, who had not even a name to share with his bride! On this memorable evening, Louis paced about by himself, crushing down the rusted fern as he strode through the wood in painful self-communion. The wind was high among the trees, and grew wild and fitful as the night advanced, bringing down showers of leaves into all the hollows, and raving with the most desolate sound in nature among the high tops of the Scotch firs, which stood grouped by themselves, a reserved and austere brotherhood, on one side of Badgeley Wood. Out of this leafy wilderness, the evening lay quiet enough upon the open fields, the wan gleams of water, and the deserted highway; but the clouds opened in a clear rift of wistful, windy, colourless sky, just over Oxford, catching with its pale half-light the mingled pinnacles and towers. Louis was too much engrossed either to see or to hear the eerie sights and sounds of the night, yet they had their influence upon him unawares.

In the mean time, and at the same moment, in the quiet country gloaming, which was odd, but by no means melancholy to him, Charlie trudged sturdily up the high-road, carrying his own little bag, and thinking his own thoughts. And down the same road, one talking a good deal, one very little, and one not at all, the three girls went to meet him, three light and graceful figures, in dim autumnal dresses—for now the evenings became somewhat cold—fit figures for this sweet half-light, which looked pleasant here, though it was so pale and ghostly in the wood. The first was Rachel, who, greatly exhilarated by her unusual freedom, and by all that had happened during these few days past, almost led the little party, protesting she was sure to know Charlie, and very near giddy in her unthinking and girlish delight. The second was Agnes, who was very thoughtful and somewhat grave, yet still could answer her companion; the third, a step behind, coming along very slow and downcast, with her veil over her drooping face, and a shadow upon her palpitating little heart, was Marian, in whose gentle mind was something very like a heavy and despondent shadow of the tumult which distracted her betrothed. Yet not that either—for there was no tumult, but only a pensive and oppressive sadness, under which the young sufferer remained very still, not caring to say a word. "What would papa say?" that was the only audible voice in Marian Atheling's heart.

"There now, I am sure it is him—there he is," cried Rachel; and it was Charlie, beyond dispute, shouldering his carpet-bag. The greeting was kindly enough, but it was not at all sentimental, which somewhat disappointed Rachel, at whom Charlie gazed with visible curiosity. When they turned with him, leading him home, Marian fell still farther back, and drooped more than ever. Perhaps the big boy was moved with a momentary sympathy—more likely it was simple mischief. "So," said Charlie in her ear, "the Yankee's cut out."

Marian started a little, looked at him eagerly, and put her hand with an appealing gesture on his arm. "Oh, Charlie, what did papa say?" asked Marian, with her heart in her eyes.

Charlie wavered for a moment between his boyish love of torture and a certain dormant tenderness at the bottom of his full man's heart, which this great event happening to Marian had touched into life all at once. The kinder sentiment prevailed after a moment's pause of wicked intention. "My father was not angry, May," said the lad; and he drew his shrinking sister's pretty hand through his own arm roughly but kindly, pleased to feel his own boyish strength a support to her. Marian was so young too— very little beyond the rapid vicissitudes of a child. She bounded forward on Charlie's arm at the words, drooping no longer, but triumphant and at ease in a moment, hurrying him up the ascending high-road at a pace which did not at all suit Charlie, and outstripping the entire party in her sudden flight to her mother with the good news. That Papa should not be angry was all that Marian desired or hoped.

At the door, in the darkness, the hasty girl ran into Mamma's arms. "My father is not angry," she exclaimed, out of breath, faithfully repeating Charlie's words; and then Marian, once more the most serviceable of domestic managers, hastened to light the candles on the tea-table, to draw the chairs around this kindly board, to warn Hannah of the approach of the heir of the house. Hannah came out into the hall to stand behind Mrs Atheling, and drop a respectful curtsy to the young gentleman. The punctilious old family attendant would have been inconsolable had she missed this opportunity of "showing her manners," and was extremely grateful to Miss Marian, who did not forget her, though she had so many things to think of of her own.

The addition of Rachel slightly embarrassed the family party, and it had the most marvellous effect upon Charlie, who had never before known any female society except that of his sisters. Charlie was full three years younger than the young stranger—distance enough to justify her in treating him as a boy, and him in conceiving the greatest admiration for her. Charlie, of all things in the world, grew actually *shy* in the company of his sisters' friend. He became afraid of committing himself, and at last began partly to believe his mother's often-repeated strictures on his "manners." He did unquestionably look so big, so *brusque*, so clumsy, beside this pretty little fairy Rachel, and his own graceful sisters. Charlie hitched up his great shoulders, retreated under the shadow of all those cloudy furrows on his brow, and had actually nothing to say. And Mrs Atheling, occupied with her husband's long and anxious letter, forbore to question him; and the girls, anxious as they still were, did not venture to say anything before

Rachel. They were not at all at their ease, and somewhat dull as they sat in the dim parlour, inventing conversation, and trying not to show their visitor that she was in the way. But she found it out at last, with a little uneasy start and blush, and hastened to get her bonnet and say good-night. No one seemed to fear that it would be difficult to find Rachel's escort, who was found accordingly the moment they appeared in the garden, starting, as he did the first time of their meeting, from the darkness of the angle at the end of the hedge. Marian ran forward to him, giving Charlie's message as it came all rosy and hopeful through the alembic of her own comforted imagination. "Papa is quite pleased," said Marian, with her smiles and her blushes. She did not perceive the suppressed vexation of Louis's brow as he tried to brighten at her news. For Marian could not have understood how this haughty and undisciplined young spirit could scarcely manage to bow itself to the approbation and judgment even of Papa.

CHAPTER XXX
A CONSULTATION

"And now, Charlie, my dear boy, I quite calculate on your knowing about it, since you have been so long at the law," said Mrs Atheling: "your father is so much taken up about other matters, that he really says very little about this. What are we to do?"

Charlie, whose mobile brow was shifting up and shifting down with all the marks of violent cogitation, bit his thumb at this, and took time before he answered it. "The first thing to be done," said Charlie, with a little dogmatism, "is to see what evidence can be had—that's what we have got to do. Has nobody found any papers of the old lady's?—she was sure to have a lot—all your old women have."

"No one even thought of looking," said Agnes, suddenly glancing up at the old cabinet with all its brass rings—while Marian, restored to all her gay spirits, promptly took her brother to task for his contempt of old women. "You ought to see Miss Anastasia—she is a great deal bigger than you," cried Marian, pulling a shaggy lock of Charlie's black hair.

"Stuff!—who's Miss Anastasia?" was the reply.

"And that reminds me," said Mrs Atheling, "that we ought to have let her know. Do you remember what she said, Agnes?—she was quite sure my lord was thinking of something—and we were to let her know."

"What about, mother?—and who's Miss Anastasia?" asked Charlie once more: he had to repeat his question several times before any answer came.

"Who is Miss Anastasia? My dear, I forgot you were a stranger. She is— well, really I cannot pretend to describe Miss Rivers," said Mrs Atheling, with a little nervousness. "I have always had a great respect for her, and so has your father. She is a very remarkable person, Charlie. I never have known any one like her all my life."

"But *who* is she, mother? Is she any good?" repeated the impatient youth.

Mrs Atheling looked at her son with a certain horror.

"She is one of the most remarkable persons in the county," said Mrs Atheling, with all the local spirit of a Banburyshire woman, born and bred—"she is a great scholar, and a lady of fortune, and the only child of the old lord. How strange the ways of Providence are, children!—what a difference it might have made in everything had Miss Anastasia been born a man instead of a woman." "Indeed," confessed Mamma, breaking off in an under-tone, "I do really believe it would have been more suitable, even for herself."

"I suppose we're to come at it at last," said Charlie despairingly: "she's a daughter of the tother lord—now, I want to know what she's got to do with us."

"My dear," said Mrs Atheling eagerly, and with evident pleasure, "I wrote to your father, I am sure, all about it. She has called upon us twice in the most friendly way, and has quite taken a liking for the girls."

"And she was old Aunt Bridget's pupil, and her great friend; and it was on account of her that the old lord gave Aunt Bridget this house," added Agnes, finding out, though not very cleverly, what Charlie's questions meant.

"And she hates Lord Winterbourne," said Marian in an expressive appendix, with a distinct emphasis of sympathy and approval on the words.

"Now I call that satisfaction," said Charlie,—"that's something like the thing. So I suppose she must have had to do with the whole business, and knows all about it—eh? Why didn't you tell me so at once?—why, she's the first person to see, of course. I had better seek her out to-morrow morning—first thing."

"You!" Mamma looked with motherly anxiety, mixed with disapproval. It was so impossible, even with the aid of all partialities, to make out Charlie to be handsome. And Miss Anastasia came of a handsome race, and had a prejudice in favour of good looks. Then, though his large loose limbs began to be a little more firmly knitted and less unmanageable, and though he was now drawing near eighteen, he was still only a boy. "My dear," said Mrs Atheling, "she is a very particular old lady, and takes dislikes sometimes, and very proud besides, and might not desire to be intruded on; and I think, after all, as you do not know her, and they do, I think it would be much better if the girls were to go."

"The girls!" exclaimed Charlie with a boy's contempt—"a great deal they know about the business! You listen to me, mother. I've been reading up hard for six months, and I know something about the evidence that does for a court of law—women don't—it's not in reason; for I'd like to see the woman that could stand old Foggo's office, pegging in at these old fellows for precedent, and all that stuff. You don't suppose I mind what your old lady thinks of me—and I know what I want, which is the main thing, after all. You tell me where she lives—that's all I want to know—and see if I don't make something of it before another day."

"Where she lives?—it is six miles off, Charlie: you don't know the way—and, indeed, you don't know her either, my poor boy."

"Don't you trouble about that—that's my business, mother," said Charlie; "and a man can't lose his way in the country unless he tries—a long road, and a fingerpost at every crossing. When a man wants to lose himself, he had better go to the City—there's no fear in your plain country roads. You set me on the right way—you know all the places hereabout—and just for this once, mother, trust me, and let me manage it my own way."

"I always did trust you, Charlie," said Mrs Atheling evasively; but she did not half like her son's enterprise, and greatly objected to put Miss Anastasia's friendship in jeopardy by such an intrusion as this.

However, the young gentleman now declared himself tired, and was conducted up-stairs in state, by his mother and sisters—first to Mrs Atheling's own room to inspect it, and kiss, half reluctantly, half with genuine fondness, the little slumbering cherub faces of Bell and Beau. Then he had a glimpse of the snowy decorations of that young-womanly and pretty apartment of his sisters, and was finally ushered into the little back-room, his own den, from which the lumber had been cleared on purpose for his reception. They left him then to his repose, and dreams, if the couch of this young gentleman was ever visited by such fairy visitants, and retired again themselves to that dim parlour, to read over in conclave Papa's letter, and hold a final consultation as to what everybody should do.

Papa's letter was very long, very anxious, and very affectionate, and had cost Papa all the leisure of two long evenings, and all his unoccupied hours for two days at the office. He blamed his wife a little, but it was very quietly,—he was grieved for the premature step the young people had taken, but did not say a great deal about his grief,—and he was extremely concerned, and evidently did not express half of his concern, about his pretty Marian, for whom he permitted himself to say he had expected a very different fate. There was not much said of personal repugnance to Louis, and little comment upon his parentage, but they could see well enough that Papa felt the matter very deeply, and that it needed all his affection for themselves, and all his charity for the stranger, to reconcile him to it. But they were both very young, he said, *and must do nothing precipitate*—which sentence Papa made very emphatic by a very black and double underscoring, and which Mrs Atheling, but fortunately not Marian, understood to mean that it was a possibility almost to be hoped for, that this might turn out one of those boy-and-girl engagements made to be broken, and never come to anything after all.

It was consolatory certainly, and set their minds at rest, but it was not a very cheering letter, and by no means justified Marian's joyful announcement that "papa was quite pleased." And so much was the good father taken up with his child's fortune, that it was only in a postscript he took any notice of Lord Winterbourne's summons and their precarious holding of the Old Wood Lodge. "We will resist, of course," said Papa. He did not know a great deal more about how to resist than they did, so he wisely left the question to Charlie, and to "another day."

And now came the question, what everybody was to do? which gradually narrowed into much smaller limits, and became wholly concerned with what Charlie was to do, and whether he should visit Miss Anastasia. He had made up his mind to it with no lack of decision. What could his mother and his sisters say, save make a virtue of necessity, and yield their assent?

CHAPTER XXXI
CHARLIE'S MISSION

Early on the next morning, accordingly, Charlie set out for Abingford. It was with difficulty he escaped a general superintendence of his toilette, and prevailed upon his mother to content herself with brushing his coat, and putting into something like arrangement the stray locks of his hair; but at last, tolerably satisfied with his appearance, and giving him many anxious instructions as to his demeanour towards Miss Anastasia, Mrs Atheling suffered him to depart upon his important errand. The road was the plainest of country roads, through the wood and over the hill, with scarcely a turn to distract the regard of the traveller. A late September morning, sunny and sweet, with yellow leaves sometimes dropping down upon the wind, and all the autumn foliage in a flush of many colours under the cool blue, and floating clouds of a somewhat dullish yet kindly sky. The deep underground of ferns, where they were not brown, were feathering away into a rich yellow, which relieved and brought out all the more strongly the harsh dark green of these vigorous fronds, rusted with seed; and piles of firewood stood here and there, tied up in big fagots, provision for the approaching winter. The birds sang gaily, still stirring among the trees; and now and then into the still air, and far-off rural hum, came the sharp report of a gun, or the ringing bark of a dog. Charlie pushed upon his way, wasting little time in observation, yet observing for all that, with the novel pleasure of a town-bred lad, and owning a certain exhilaration in his face, and in his breast, as he sped along the country road, with its hedges and strips of herbage; that straight, clear, even road, with its milestones and fingerposts, and one market-cart coming along in leisurely rural fashion, half a mile off upon the far-seen way. The walk to Abingford was a long walk even for Charlie, and it was nearly an hour and a half from the time of his leaving home, when he began to perceive glimpses through the leaves of a little maze of water, two or three streams, splitting into fantastic islands the houses and roofs before him, and came in sight of an old gateway, with two windows and a high peaked roof over it, which strode across the way. Charlie, who was entirely unacquainted with such peculiarities of architecture, made a pause of half-contemptuous boyish observation, looking up at the windows, and supposing it must be rather odd to live over an archway. Then he bethought him of asking a loitering country lad to direct him to the Priory, which was done in the briefest manner possible, by pointing round the side of the gate to a large door which almost seemed to form part of it. "There it be," said Charlie's informant, and Charlie immediately made his assault upon the big door.

Miss Rivers was at home. He was shown into a large dim room full of books, with open windows, and green blinds let down to the floor, through which the visitor could only catch an uncertain glimpse of waving branches, and a lawn which sloped to the pale little river: the room was hung with portraits, which there was not light enough to see, and gave back a dull glimmer from the glass of its great bookcases. There was a large writing-table before the fireplace, and a great easy-chair placed by it. This was where Miss Anastasia transacted business; but Charlie had not much time, if he had inclination, for a particular survey of the apartment, for he could hear a quick and decided step descending a stair, as it seemed, and crossing over the hall. "Charles Atheling—who's *Charles* Atheling?" said a peremptory voice outside. "I know no one of the name."

With the words on her lips Miss Anastasia entered the room. She wore a loose morning-dress, belted round her waist with a buckled girdle, and a big tippet of the same; and her cap, which was not intended to be pretty, but only to be comfortable, came down close over her ears, snow white, and of the finest cambric, but looking very homely and familiar indeed to the puzzled eyes of Charlie. Not her homely cap, however, nor her odd dress, could make Miss Anastasia less imperative or formidable. "Well sir," she said, coming in upon him without very much ceremony, "which of the Athelings do you belong to, and what do you want with me?"

"I belong to the Old Wood Lodge," said Charlie, almost as briefly, "and I want to ask what you know about it, and how it came into Aunt Bridget's hands."

"What I know about it? Of course I know everything about it," said Miss Anastasia. "So you're young Atheling, are you? You're not at all like your pretty sisters; not clever either, so far as I can see, eh? What are you good for, boy?"

Charlie did not say "stuff!" aloud, but it was only by a strong effort of self-control. He was not at all disposed to give any answer to the question. "What has to be done in the mean time is to save my father's property," said Charlie, with a boyish flush of offence.

"Save it, boy! who's threatening your father's property? What! do you mean to tell me already that he's fallen foul of Will Atheling?" said the old lady, drawing her big easy-chair to her big writing-table, and motioning Charlie to draw near. "Eh? why don't you speak? tell me the whole at once."

"Lord Winterbourne has sent us notice to leave," said Charlie; "he says the Old Wood Lodge was only Aunt Bridget's for life, and is his now. I have set the girls to look up the old lady's papers; we ourselves know nothing about it, and I concluded the first thing to be done was to come and ask you."

"Good," said Miss Anastasia; "you were perfectly right. Of course it is a lie."

This was said perfectly in a matter-of-course fashion, without the least idea, apparently, on the part of the old lady, that there was anything astonishing in the lie which came from Lord Winterbourne.

"I know everything about it," she continued; "my father made over the little house to my dear old professor, when we supposed she would have occasion to leave me: *that* turned out a vain separation, thanks to *him* again;" and here Miss Rivers grew white for an instant, and pressed her lips together. "Please Heaven, my boy, he'll not be successful this time. No. I know everything about it; we'll foil my lord in this."

"But there must have been a deed," said Charlie; "do you know where the papers are?"

"Papers! I tell you I am acquainted with every circumstance—I myself. You can call me as a witness," said the old lady. "No, I can't tell you where the papers are. What's about them? eh? Do you mean to say they are of more consequence than me?"

"There are sure to be documents on the other side," said Charlie; "the original deed would settle the question, without needing even a trial: without it Lord Winterbourne has the better chance. Personal testimony is not equal to documents in a case like this."

"Young Atheling," said Miss Rivers, drawing herself up to her full height, "do you think a jury of this county would weigh *his* word against mine?"

Charlie was considerably embarrassed. "I suppose not," he said, somewhat abruptly; "but this is not a thing of words. Lord Winterbourne will never appear at all; but if he has any papers to produce proving his case, the matter will be settled at once; and unless we have counterbalancing evidence of the same kind, we'd better give it up before it comes that length."

He said this half impatient, half despairing. Miss Rivers evidently took up this view of the question with dissatisfaction; but as he persevered in it, came gradually to turn her thoughts to other means of assisting him. "But I know of no papers," she said, with disappointment; "my father's solicitor, to be sure, he is the man to apply to. I shall make a point of seeing him to-morrow; and what papers I have I will look over. By the by, now I remember it, the Old Wood Lodge belonged to her grandfather or great-grandfather, dear old soul, and came to us by some mortgage or forfeit. It was given back—*restored*, not bestowed upon her. For her life!—I should like to find out now what he means by such a lie!"

Charlie, who could throw no light upon this subject, rose to go, somewhat disappointed, though not at all discouraged. The old lady stopped him on his way, carried him off to another room, and administered, half against Charlie's will, a glass of wine. "Now, young Atheling, you can go," said Miss Anastasia. "I'll remember both you and your business. What are they bringing you up to? eh?"

"I'm in a solicitor's office," said Charlie.

"Just so—quite right," said Miss Anastasia. "Let me see you baffle *him*, and I'll be your first client. Now go away to your pretty sisters, and tell your mother not to alarm herself. I'll come to the Lodge in a day or two; and if there's documents to be had, you shall have them. Under any circumstances," continued the old lady, dismissing him with a certain stateliness, "you can call *me*."

But though she was a great lady, and the most remarkable person in the county, Charlie did not appreciate this permission half so much as he would have appreciated some bit of wordy parchment. He walked back again, much less sure of his case than when he set out with the hope of finding all he wanted at Abingford.

CHAPTER XXXII
SEARCH

When Charlie reached home again, very tired, and in a somewhat moody frame of mind, he found the room littered with various old boxes undergoing examination, and Agnes seated before the cabinet, with a lapful of letters, and her face bright with interest and excitement, looking them over. At the present moment, she held something of a very perplexing nature in her hand, which the trained eye of Charlie caught instantly, with a flash of triumph. Agnes herself was somewhat excited about it, and Marian stood behind her, looking over her shoulder, and vainly trying to decipher the ancient writing. "It's something, mamma," cried Agnes. "I am sure, if Charlie saw it, he would think it something; but I cannot make out what it is. Here is somebody's seal and somebody's signature, and there, I am sure, that is Atheling; and a date, 'xiij. of May, M.D.LXXII.' What does that mean, Marian? M. a thousand, D. five hundred; there it is! I am sure it is an old deed—a real something ancestral—1572!"

"Give it to me," said Charlie, stretching his hand for it over her shoulder. No one had heard him come in.

"Oh, Charlie, what did Miss Anastasia say?" cried Marian; and Agnes immediately turned round away from the cabinet, and Mamma laid down her work. Charlie, however, took full time to examine the yellow old document they had found, though he did not acknowledge that it posed him scarcely less than themselves, before he spoke.

"She said she'd look up her papers, and speak to the old gentleman's solicitor. I don't see that *she's* much good to us," said Charlie. "She says I might call her as a witness, but what's the good of a witness against documents? This has nothing to do with Aunt Bridget, Agnes—have you found nothing more than this? Why, you know there must have been a deed of some kind. The old lady could not have been so foolish as to throw away her title. Property without title-deeds is not worth a straw; and the man that drew up her will is my lord's solicitor! I say, he must be what the Yankees call a smart man, this Lord Winterbourne."

"I am afraid he has no principle, my dear," said Mrs Atheling with a sigh.

"And a very bad man—everybody hates him," said Marian under her breath.

She spoke so low that she did not receive that reproving look of Mamma which was wont to check such exclamations. Marian, though she had a will of her own, and was never like to fall into a mere shadow and reflection of her lover, as his poor little sister did, had unconsciously imbibed Louis's sentiments. She did not know what it was to *hate*, this innocent girl. Had she seen Lord Winterbourne thrown from his horse, or overturned out of his carriage, these ferocious sentiments would have melted in an instant into help and pity; but in the abstract view of the matter, Marian pronounced with emotion the great man's sentence, "Everybody hates Lord Winterbourne."

"That is what the old lady said," exclaimed Charlie; "she asked me who I thought would believe him against her? But that's not the question. I don't want to pit one man against another. My father's worth twenty of Lord Winterbourne! But that's no matter. The law cares nothing at all for his principles. What title has he got, and what title have you?—that's what the law's got to say. Now, I'll either have something to put in against him or I'll not plead. It's no use taking a step in the matter without proof."

"And won't that do, Charlie?" asked Mrs Atheling, looking wistfully at the piece of parchment, signed and sealed, which was in Charlie's hands.

"That! why, it's two hundred and fifty years old!" said Charlie. "I don't see what it refers to yet, but it's very clear it can't be to Miss Bridget. No, mother, that won't do."

"Then, my dear," said Mrs Atheling, "I am very sorry to think of it; but, after all, we have not been very long here, and we might have laid out more money, and formed more attachments to the place, if we had gone on much longer; and I think I shall be very glad to get back to Bellevue. Marian, my love, don't cry; this need not make any difference with *anything*; but I think it is far better just to make up our minds to it, and give up the Old Wood Lodge."

"Mother! do you think I mean that?" cried Charlie; "we must find the papers, that's what we must do. My father's as good an Englishman as the first lord in the kingdom; I'd not give in to the king unless he was in the right."

"And not even then, unless you could not help it," said Agnes, laughing; "but I am not half done yet; there is still a great quantity of letters—and I should not be at all surprised if this romantic old cabinet, like an old bureau in a novel, had a secret drawer."

Animated by this idea, Marian ran to the antique little piece of furniture, pressing every projection with her pretty fingers, and examining into every creak. But there was no secret drawer—a fact which became all the more apparent when a drawer *was* discovered, which once had closed with a spring. The spring was broken, and the once-secret place was open, desolate, and empty. Miss Bridget, good old lady, had no secrets, or at least she had not made any provision for them here.

Agnes went on with her examination the whole afternoon, drawn aside and deluded to pursue the history of old Aunt Bridget's life through scores of yellow old letters, under the pretence that something might be found in some of them to throw light upon this matter; for a great many letters of Miss Bridget's own—careful "studies" for the production itself—were tied up among the others; and it would have been amusing, if it had not been sad, to sit on this little eminence of time, looking over that strange faithful self-record of the little weaknesses, the ladylike pretences, the grand Johnsonian diction of the old lady who was dead. Poor old lady! Agnes became quite abashed and ashamed of herself when she felt a smile stealing over her lip. It seemed something like profanity to ransack the old cabinet, and smile at it. In its way, this, as truly as the grass-mound, in Winterbourne churchyard, was Aunt Bridget's grave.

But still nothing could be found. Charlie occupied himself during the remainder of the day in giving a necessary notice to Mr Lewis the solicitor, that they had made up their minds to resist Lord Winterbourne's claim; and when the evening closed in, and the candles were lighted, Louis made his first public appearance since the arrival of the stranger, somewhat cloudy, and full of all his old haughtiness. This cloud vanished in an instant at the first glance. Whatever Charlie's qualities were, criticism was not one of them; it was clear that though his "No" might be formidable enough of itself, Charlie had not been a member of any solemn committee, sitting upon the pretensions of Louis. He gave no particular regard to Louis even now, but sat poring over the old deed, deciphering it with the most patient laboriousness, with his head very close over the paper, and a pair of spectacles assisting his eyes. The spectacles were lent by Mamma, who kept them, not secretly, but with a little reserve, in her work-basket, for special occasions when she had some very fine stitching to do, or was busy with delicate needlework by candle-light; and nothing could have been more oddly inappropriate to the face of Charlie, with all the furrows of his brow rolled down over his eyebrows, and his indomitable upper-lip pressed hard upon its fellow, than these same spectacles. Then they made him short-sighted, and were only of use when he leaned closely over the paper—Charlie did not mind, though his shoulders ached and his eyes filled with water. He was making it out!

And Agnes, for her part, sat absorbed with her lapful of old letters, reading them all over with passing smiles and gravities, growing into acquaintance with ever so many extinct affairs,—old stories long ago come to the one conclusion which unites all men. Though she felt herself virtuously reading for a purpose, she had forgotten all about the purpose long ago, and was only wandering on and on by a strange attraction, as if through a city of the dead. But it was quite impossible to think of the dead among these yellow old papers—the littlest trivial things of life were so quite living in them, in these unconscious natural inferences and implications. And Louis and Marian, sometimes speaking and often silent, were going through their own present romance and story; and Mamma, in her sympathetic middle age, with her work-basket, was tenderly overlooking all. In the little dim country parlour, lighted with the two candles, what a strange epitome there was of a whole world and a universal life.

CHAPTER XXXIII
DOUBTS AND FEARS

Louis had not been told till this day of the peril which threatened the little inheritance of the Athelings. When he did hear of it, the young man gnashed his teeth with that impotent rage which is agony, desperate under the oppression which makes even wise men mad. He scorned to say a word of any further indignities put upon himself; but Rachel told of them with tears and outcries almost hysterical—how my lord had challenged him with bitter taunts to put on his livery and earn the bread he ate—how he had been expelled from his room which he had always occupied, and had an apartment now among the rooms of the servants—and how Lord Winterbourne threatened to advertise him publicly as a vagabond and runaway if he ventured beyond the bounds of the village, or tried to thrust himself into any society. Poor little Rachel, when she came in the morning faint and heart-broken to tell her story, could scarcely speak for tears, and was only with great difficulty soothed to a moderate degree of calm. But still she shrank with the strangest repugnance from going away. It scarcely could be attachment to the home of her youth, for it had always been an unhappy shelter—nor could it be love for any of the family; the little timid spirit feared she knew not what terrors in the world with which she had so little acquaintance. Lord Winterbourne to her was not a mere English peer, of influence only in a certain place and sphere, but an omnipotent oppressor, from whose power it would be impossible to escape, and whose vigilance could not be eluded. If she tried to smile at the happy devices of Agnes and Marian, how to establish herself in their own room at Bellevue, and lodge Louis close at hand, it was a very wan and sickly smile. She confessed it was dreadful to think that he should remain, exposed to all these insults; but she shrank with fear and trembling from the idea of Louis going away.

The next evening, just before the sun set, the whole youthful party— for Rachel, by a rare chance, was not to be "wanted" to-night—strayed along the grassy road in a body towards the church. Agnes and Marian were both with Louis, who had been persuaded at last to speak of his own persecutions, while Rachel came behind with Charlie, kindly pointing out for him the far-off towers of Oxford, the two rivers wandering in a maze, and all the features of the scene which Charlie did not know, and amused, sad as she was, in her conscious seniority and womanhood, at the shyness of the lad. Charlie actually began to be touched with a wandering breath of sentiment, had been seen within the last two days reading a poetry book, and was really in a very odd and suspicious "way."

"No," said Louis, upon whom his betrothed and her sister were hanging eagerly, comforting and persuading—"no; I am not in a worse position. It stings me at the moment, I confess; but I am filled with contempt for the man who insults me, and his words lose their power. I could almost be seduced to stay when he begins to struggle with me after this downright fashion; but you are perfectly right for all that, and within a few days I must go away."

"A few days? O Louis!" cried Marian, clinging to his arm.

"Yes; I have a good mind to say to-morrow, to enhance my own value," said Louis. "I am tempted—ay, both to go and stay—for sake of the clinging of these little hands. Never mind, our mother will come home all the sooner; and what do you suppose I will do?"

"I think indeed, Louis, you should speak to the Rector," said Agnes, with a little anxiety. "O no; it is very cruel of you, and you are quite wrong; he did not mean to be very kind in that mocking way—he meant what he said—he wanted to do you service; and so he would, and vindicate you when you were gone, if you only would cease to be so very grand for two minutes, and let him know."

"Am I so very grand?" said Louis, with a momentary pique. "I have nothing to do with your rectors—I know what he meant, whatever he might say."

"It is a great deal more than he does himself, I am sure of that," said Agnes with a puzzled air. "He means what he says, but he does not always know what he means; and neither do I."

Marian tried a trembling little laugh at her sister's perplexity, but they were rather too much moved for laughing, and it did not do.

"Now, I will tell you what my plan is," said Louis. "I do not know what he thinks of me, nor do I expect to find his opinion very favourable; but as that is all I can look for anywhere, it will be the better probation for me," he added, with a rising colour and an air of haughtiness. "I will not enlist, Marian. I have no longer any dreams of the marshal's *baton* in the soldier's knapsack. I give up rank and renown to those who can strive for them. You must be content with such honour as a man can have in his own person, Marian. When I leave you, I will go at once to your father."

"Oh, Louis, will you? I am so glad, so proud!" and again the little hands pressed his arm, and Marian looked up to him with her radiant face. He had not felt before how perfectly magnanimous and noble his resolution was.

"I think it will be very right," said Agnes, who was not so enthusiastic; "and my father will be pleased to see you, Louis, though you doubt him as you doubt all men. But look, who is this coming here?"

They were scarcely coming here, seeing they were standing still under the porch of the church, a pair of very tall figures, very nearly equal in altitude, though much unlike each other. One of them was the Rector, who stood with a solemn bored look at the door of his church, which he had just closed, listening, without any answer save now and then a grave and ceremonious bow, to the other "individual," who was talking very fluently, and sufficiently loud to be heard by others than the Rector. "Oh, Agnes!" cried Marian, and "Hush, May!" answered her sister; they both recognised the stranger at a glance.

"Yes, this is the pride of the old country," said the voice; "here, sir, we can still perceive upon the sands of time the footprints of our Saxon ancestors. I say ours, for my youthful and aspiring nation boasts as the brightest star in her banner the Anglo-Saxon blood. *We* preserve the free institutions—the hatred of superstition, the freedom of private judgment and public opinion, the great inheritance developed out of the past; but Old England, sir, a land which I venerate, yet pity, keeps safe in her own bosom the external traces full of instruction, the silent poetry of Time—that only poetry which she can refuse to share with us."

To this suitable and appropriate speech, congenial as it must have been to his feelings, the Rector made no answer, save that most deferential and solemn bow, and was proceeding with a certain conscientious haughtiness to show his visitor some other part of the building, when his eye was attracted by the approaching group. He turned to them immediately with an air of sudden relief.

So did Mr Endicott, to whom, to do him justice, not all the old churches in Banburyshire, nor all the opportunities of speechmaking, nor even half-a-dozen rectors who were within two steps of a peerage, could have presented such powerful attractions as did that beautiful blushing face of Marian Atheling, drooping and falling back under the shadow of Louis. The Yankee hastened forward with his best greeting.

"When I remember our last meeting," said Mr Endicott, bending his thin head forward with the most unusual deference, that tantalising vision of what might have been, "I think myself fortunate indeed to have found you so near your home. I have been visiting your renowned city—one of those twins of learning, whose antiquity is its charm. In my country our antiquities stretch back into the eternities; but we know nothing of the fourteenth or the fifteenth century in our young soil. My friend the Rector has been showing me his church."

Mr Endicott's friend the Rector stared at him with a haughty amazement, but came forward without saying anything to the new-comers; then he seemed to pause a moment, doubtful how to address Louis—a doubt which the young man solved for him instantly by taking off his hat with an exaggerated and solemn politeness. They bowed to each other loftily, these two haughty young men, as two duellists might have saluted each other over their weapons. Then Louis turned his fair companion gently, and, without saying anything, led her back again on the road they had just traversed. Agnes followed silently, and feeling very awkward, with the Rector and Mr Endicott on either hand. The Rector did not say a word. Agnes only answered in shy monosyllables. The gifted American had it all his own way.

"I understand Viscount Winterbourne and Mrs Edgerley are at Winterbourne Hall," said Mrs Endicott. "She is a charming person; the union of a woman of fashion and a woman of literature is one so rarely seen in this land."

"Yes," said Agnes, who knew nothing else to say.

"For myself," said Mr Endicott solemnly, "I rejoice to find the poetic gift alike in the palace of the peer and the cottage of the peasant, bringing home to all hearts the experiences of life; in the sumptuous apartments of the Hall with Mrs Edgerley, or in the humble parlour of the worthy and respectable middle class—Miss Atheling, with you."

"Oh!" cried Agnes, starting under this sudden blow, and parrying it with all the skill she could find. "Do you like Oxford, Mr Endicott? Have you seen much of the country about here?"

But it was too late. Mr Endicott caught a shy backward glance of Marian, and, smothering a mortal jealousy of Louis, eagerly thrust himself forward to answer it—and the Rector had caught his unfortunate words. The Rector drew himself up to a still more lofty height, if that was possible, and walked on by Agnes's side in a solemn and stately silence—poor Agnes, who would have revived a little in his presence but for that arrow of Mr Endicott's, not knowing whether to address him, or whether her best policy was to be silent. She went on by his side, holding down her head, looking very small, very slight, very young, beside that dignified and stately personage. At last he himself condescended to speak.

"Am I to understand, Miss Atheling," said the Rector, very much in the same tone as he might have asked poor little Billy Morrell at school, "Are you the boy who robbed John Parker's orchard?"—"Am I to understand, as I should be disposed to conclude from what this person says, that, like my fashionable cousin at the Hall, you have written novels?—or is it only the hyperbole of that individual's ordinary speech?"

"No," said Agnes, very guilty, a convicted culprit, yet making bold to confess her guilt. "I am very sorry he said it, but it is true; only I have written just one novel. Do you think it wrong?"

"I think a woman's intellect ought to be receptive without endeavouring to produce," said the Rector, in a slightly acerbated tone. "Intelligence is the noblest gift of a woman; originality is neither to be wished nor looked for."

"I do not suppose I am very guilty of that either," said Agnes, brightening again with that odd touch of pugnacity, as she listened once more to this haughty tone of dogmatism from the man who held no opinions. "If you object only to originality, I do not think you need be angry with me."

She was half inclined to play with the lion, but the lion was in a very ill humour, and would see no sport in the matter. To tell the truth, the Rector was very much fretted by this unlooked-for intelligence. He felt as if it were done on purpose, and meant as a personal offence to him, though really, after all, for a superior sister of St Frideswide, this unfortunate gift of literature was rather a recommendation than otherwise, as one might have thought.

So the Rev. Lionel Rivers stalked on beside Agnes past his own door, following Louis, Marian, and Mr Endicott to the very gate of the Old Wood Lodge. Then he took off his hat to them all, wished them a ceremonious good-night, and went home extremely wrathful, and in a most unpriestly state of mind. He could not endure to think that the common outer world had gained such a hold upon that predestined Superior of the sisters of St Frideswide.

CHAPTER XXXIV
SOME PROGRESS

After a long and most laborious investigation of the old parchment, Charlie at last triumphantly made it out to be an old conveyance, to a remote ancestor, of this very little house, and sundry property adjoining, on which the Athelings had now no claim. More than two hundred and fifty years ago!—the girls were as much pleased with it as if it had been an estate, and even Charlie owned a thrill of gratification. They felt themselves quite long-descended and patrician people, in right of the ancestor who had held "the family property" in 1572.

But it was difficult to see what use this could be of in opposition to the claim of Lord Winterbourne. Half the estates in the country at least had changed hands during these two hundred and fifty years; and though it certainly proved beyond dispute that the Old Wood Lodge had once been the property of the Athelings, it threw no light whatever on the title of Miss Bridget. Mrs Atheling looked round upon the old walls with much increase of respect; she wondered if they really could be so old as that; and was quite reverential of her little house, being totally unacquainted with the periods of domestic architecture, and knowing nothing whatever of archaic "detail."

Miss Anastasia, however, remembered her promise. Only two or three days after Charlie's visit to her, the two grey ponies made their appearance once more at the gate of the Old Wood Lodge. She was not exactly triumphant, but had a look of satisfaction on her face, and evidently felt she had gained something. She entered upon her business without a moment's delay.

"Young Atheling, I have brought you all that Mr Temple can furnish me with," said Miss Anastasia—"his memorandum taken from my father's instructions. He tells me there was a deed distinct and formal, and offers to bear his witness of it, as I have offered mine."

Charlie took eagerly out of her hand the paper she offered to him. "It is a copy out of his book," said Miss Anastasia. It was headed thus: "*Mem.*—To convey to Miss Bridget Atheling, her heirs and assigns, the cottage called the

Old Wood Lodge, with a certain piece of land adjoining, to be described—partly as a proof of Lord Winterbourne's gratitude for services, partly as restoring property acquired by his father—to be executed at once."

The date was five-and-twenty years ago; and perhaps nothing but justice to her dead friend and to her living ones could have fortified Miss Anastasia to return upon that time. She sat still, looking at Charlie while he read it, with her cheek a little blanched and her eye brighter than usual. He laid it down with a look of impatience, yet satisfaction. "Some one," said Charlie, "either for one side or for the other side, must have this deed."

"Your boy is hard to please," said Miss Rivers. "I have offered to appear myself, and so does Mr Temple. What, boy, not content!"

"It is the next best," said Charlie; "but still not so good as the deed; and the deed must exist somewhere; nobody would destroy such a thing. Where is it likely to be?"

"Young Atheling," said Miss Anastasia, half amused, half with displeasure, "when I want to collect evidence, you shall do it for me. Has he had a good education?—eh?"

"To *you* I am afraid he will seem a very poor scholar," said Mrs Atheling, with a little awe of Miss Anastasia's learning; "but we did what we could for him; and he has always been a very industrious boy, and has studied a good deal himself."

To this aside conversation Charlie paid not the smallest attention, but ruminated over the lawyer's memorandum, making faces at it, and bending all the powers of his mind to the consideration—where to find this deed! "If it's not here, nor in her lawyer's, nor with this old lady, *he's* got it," pronounced Charlie; but this was entirely a private process, and he did not say a word aloud.

"I've read her book," said Miss Rivers, with a glance aside at Agnes; "it's a very clever book: I approve of it, though I never read novels: in my day, girls did no such things—all the better for them now. Yes, my child, don't be afraid. I'll not call you unfeminine—in my opinion, it's about the prettiest kind of fancy-work a young woman can do."

Under this applause Agnes smiled and brightened; it was a great deal more agreeable than all the pretty sayings of all the people who were dying to know the author of *Hope Hazlewood*, in the brief day of her reputation at the Willows.

"And as for the pretty one," said Miss Anastasia, "she, I suppose, contents herself with lovers—eh? What is the meaning of this? I suppose the child's heart is in it. The worse for her—the worse for her!"

For Marian had blushed deeply, and then become very pale; her heart was touched indeed, and she was very despondent. All the other events of the time were swallowed up to Marian by one great shadow—Louis was going away!

Whereupon Mrs Atheling, unconsciously eager to attract the interest of Miss Anastasia, who very likely would be kind to the young people, sent Marian up-stairs upon a hastily-invented errand, and took the old lady aside to tell her what had happened. Miss Rivers was a good deal surprised—a little affected. "So—so—so," she said slowly, "these reckless young creatures—how ready they are to plunge into all the griefs of life! And what does Will Atheling say to this nameless boy?"

"I cannot say my husband is entirely pleased," said Mrs Atheling, with a little hesitation; "but he is a very fine young man; and to see our children happy is the great thing we care for, both William and me."

"How do you know it will make her happy?" asked Miss Anastasia somewhat sharply. "The child flushes and pales again, pretty creature as she is, like a woman come into her troubles. A great deal safer to write novels! But what is done can't be undone; and I am glad to hear of it on account of the boy."

Then Miss Anastasia made a pause, thinking over the matter. "I have found some traces of my father's wanderings," she said again, with a little emotion: "if the old man was tempted to sin in his old days, though it would be a shame to hear of, I should still be glad to make sure; and if by any chance," continued the old lady, reddening with the maidenly and delicate feeling of which her fifty years could not deprive her—"if by any chance these unfortunate children should turn out to be nearly related to me, I will of course think it my duty to provide for them as if they were lawful children of my father's house."

It cost her a little effort to say this—and Mrs Atheling, not venturing to make any comment, looked on with respectful sympathy. It was very well for Miss Anastasia to say, but how far Louis would tolerate a provision made for him was quite a different question. The silence was broken again by the old lady herself.

"This bold boy of yours has set me to look over all my old papers," said Miss Anastasia, with a twinkle of satisfaction and amusement in her eye, as she looked over at Charlie, still making faces at the lawyer's note. "Now that I have begun for *her* sake, dear old soul, I continue for my own, and for curiosity: I would give a great deal to find out the story of these children. Young Atheling, if I some time want your services, will you give them to me?"

Charlie looked up with a boyish flush of pleasure. "As soon as this business is settled," said Charlie. Miss Anastasia, whom his mother feared to look at lest she should be offended, smiled approvingly; patted the shoulder of Agnes as she passed her, left "her love for the other poor child," and went away. Mrs Atheling looked after her with a not unnatural degree of complacency. "Now, I think it very likely indeed that she will either leave them something, or try what she can do for Louis," said Mamma; she did not think how impossible it would be to do anything for Louis, until Louis graciously accepted the service; nor indeed, that the only thing the young man could do under his circumstances was to trust to his own exertions solely, and seek service from none.

CHAPTER XXXV
A GREAT DISCOVERY

The visit of Miss Rivers was an early one, some time before their mid-day dinner; and the day went on quietly after its usual fashion, and fell into the stillness of a sunny afternoon, which looked like a reminiscence of midsummer among these early October days. Mrs Atheling sat in her big chair, knitting, with a little drowsiness, a little stocking—though this was a branch of art in which Hannah was found to excel, and had begged her mistress to leave to her. Agnes sat at the table with her blotting-book, busy with her special business; Charlie was writing out a careful copy of the old deed. The door was open, and Bell and Beau, under the happy charge of Rachel, ran back and forwards, out and in, from the parlour to the garden, not omitting now and then a visit to the kitchen, where Hannah, covered all over with her white bib and apron, was making cakes for tea. Their merry childish voices and prattling feet gave no disturbance to the busy people in the parlour; neither did the light fairy step of Rachel, nor even the songs she sang to them in her wonderful voice—they were all so well accustomed to its music now. Marian and Louis, who did not like to lose sight of each other in these last days, were out wandering about the fields, or in the wood, thinking of little in the world except each other, and that great uncertain future which Louis penetrated with his fiery glances, and of which Marian wept and smiled to hear. Mamma sitting at the window, between the pauses of her knitting and the breaks of her gentle drowsiness, looked out for them with a little tender anxiety. Marian, the only one of her children who was "in trouble," was nearest of all at that moment to her mother's heart.

When suddenly a violent sound of wheels from the high-road broke in upon the stillness, then a loud voice calling to horses, and then a dull plunge and heavy roll. Mrs Atheling lifted her startled eyes, drowsy no longer, to see what was the matter, just in time to behold, what shook the little house like the shock of a small earthquake, Miss Anastasia's two grey horses, trembling with unusual exertion, draw up with a bound and commotion at the little gate.

And before the good mother could rise to her feet, wondering what could be the cause of this second visit, Miss Rivers herself sprang out of the carriage, and came into the house like a wind, almost stumbling over Rachel, and nearly upsetting Bell and Beau. She did not say a word to either mother or daughter, she only came to the threshold of the parlour, waved her hand imperiously, and cried, "Young Atheling, I want *you!*"

Charlie was not given to rapid movements, but there was no misunderstanding the extreme emotion of this old lady. The big boy got up at once and followed her, for she went out again immediately. Then Mrs Atheling, sitting at the window in amaze, saw her son and Miss Anastasia stand together in the garden, conversing with great earnestness. She showed him a book, which Charlie at first did not seem to understand, to the great impatience of his companion. Mrs Atheling drew back troubled, and in the most utter astonishment—what could it mean?

"Young Atheling," said Miss Anastasia abruptly, "I want you to give up this business of your father's immediately, and set off to Italy on mine. I have made a discovery of the most terrible importance: though you are only a boy I can trust you. Do you hear me?—it is to bring to his inheritance my father's son!"

Charlie looked up in her face astonished, and without comprehension. "My father's business is of importance to us," he said, with a momentary sullenness.

"So it is; my own man of business shall undertake it; but I want an agent, secret and sure, who is not like to be suspected," said Miss Anastasia. "Young Atheling, look here!"

Charlie looked, but not with enthusiasm. The book she handed him was an old diary of the most commonplace description, each page divided with red lines into compartments for three days, with printed headings for Monday, Tuesday, Wednesday, and so on, and columns for money. The wind fluttered the leaves, so that the only entry visible to Charlie was one relating to some purchase, which he read aloud, bewildered and wondering. Miss Anastasia, who was extremely moved and excited, looked furious, and as if she was almost tempted to administer personal chastisement to the blunderer. She turned over the fluttered leaves with an impetuous gesture. "Look here," she said, pointing to the words with her imperative finger, and reading them aloud in a low, restrained, but most emphatic voice. The entry was in the same hand, duly dated under the red line—"Twins—one boy—and Giulietta safe. Thank God. My sweet young wife."

"Now go—fly!" cried Miss Anastasia, "find out their birthday, and then come to me for money and directions. I will make your fortune, boy; you shall be the richest pettifogger in Christendom. Do you hear me, young

Atheling—do you hear me! He is the true Lord Winterbourne—he is my father's lawful son!"

To say that Charlie was not stunned by this sudden suggestion, or that there was no answer of young and generous enthusiasm, as well as of professional eagerness in his mind, to the address of Miss Rivers, would have been to do him less than justice. "Is it Italy?—I don't know a word of Italian," cried Charlie. "Never mind, I'll go to-morrow. I can learn it on the way."

The old lady grasped the boy's rough hand, and stepped again into her carriage. "Let it be to-morrow," she said, speaking very low; "tell your mother, but no one else, and do not, for any consideration, let it come to the ears of Louis—Louis, my father's boy!—But I will not see him, Charlie; fly, boy, as if you had wings!—till you come home. I will meet you to-morrow at Mr Temple's office—you know where that is—at twelve o'clock. Be ready to go immediately, and tell your mother to mention it to no creature till I see her again."

Saying which, Miss Rivers turned her ponies, Charlie hurried into the house, and his mother sat gazing out of the window, with the most blank and utter astonishment. Miss Anastasia had not a glance to spare for the watcher, and took no time to pull her rose from the porch. She drove home again at full speed, solacing her impatience with the haste of her progress, and repeating, under her breath, again and again, the same words. "One boy—and Giulietta safe. My sweet young wife!"